UNLEASHING PRODUCTIVITY

UNLEASHING PRODUCTIVITY

Prescription for Manufacturing Survival

Tim Fleskes

Copyright @ 2025 by Tim Fleskes
Second Edition, Published by Lynx Publishers, 2025
First Edition, printing by Gann Publishing Company, 1995

All Rights Reserved.

Reproduction or translation of any part of this work beyond that permitted by Section 107 or 108 of the 1976 United States Copyright Act without the written permission of the copyright owner is unlawful. Requests for permission or further information should be addressed to:

>   Permissions Department
>   Lynx Publishers
>   15728 Lorain Avenue
>   Cleveland, Ohio 44111

This publication is designed to provide accurate and authoritative information in regard to the subject matter covered. It is sold with the understanding that the publisher is not engaged in rendering legal, accounting, or other professional services. If legal advice or other professional assistance is required, the services of a competent professional person should be sought. *From a Declaration of Principles jointly adopted by a Committee of the American Bar Association and a Committee of Publishers.*

ISBN eBook: 978-1-968012-01-4
ISBN Paperback: 978-1-968012-02-1
ISBN Hardcover: 978-1-968012-03-8
ISBN Audiobook: 978-1-968012-04-5

Library Of Congress Catalog Card Number: 2025912543

Published in the United States of America.

UNLEASHING PRODUCTIVITY
PRESCRIPTION FOR MANUFACTURING SURVIVAL

IS

About improving your manufacturing productivity by implementing currently available manufacturing technologies, to produce high quality marketable products, at a better price.

The author shows how to clearly identify and evaluate economic, strategic, and other variables that impact capital investment decisions. Being more competitive in the marketplace and improving return on investment are just two of the benefits you can gain. Learn how to identify the many opportunities (often disguised as problems) that can make your enterprise more productive and profitable. Actual examples of advanced metal removal, fabrication, and robotic welding systems (RWS) proposals that have been approved and implemented, and are now operational and proven, are included. Logical arguments that you can use to help justify major capital investment programs.

Many standard industry concepts are discussed in detail such as Thruput, Utilization, Productivity, Program Justification, Automation and Robotics, Return On Investment (ROI), Net Present Value (NPV), and Make Or Buy decisions.

Required reading for: Equipment Builders, Production Managers, Manufacturing Engineers, Equipment Sellers, Finance People, Executives, Educators, and Students.

- A challenge to manufacturing for improved productivity.
- A comprehensive work on the contribution of capital to productivity improvement.
- A guide for program justification.

HOW TO BECOME AND STAY NUMBER ONE!

To my Father and Mother . . .

>*Without whose love, guidance, encouragement, and support, this book would never have made it.*

>*May they rest in peace.*

And my five children. . .

>*Kay, Ann, Damian, Peter, and Benjamin.*

They would be very proud.

Special Thanks . . .

To my wife Dorothea, my children, and my friend Nick whose patience and encouragement helped so much to make this book happen.

And, to all those who contributed so positively with their comments and critiques on the ideas, drafts and manuscripts prior to this printing.

You are all very special people.

Thank you.

And more Special Thanks to . . .

Kay Frances Fleskes (Daughter)

Jordan Theilsen Berger (Grandson)

For all their contributions and help in getting this Second Edition off the ground.

Acknowledgements . . .

To the many people who have contributed and sacrificed for the success of the productivity improvement projects that I have been fortunate enough to be involved in . . . **Thank You!**

First, to the people whose jobs disappeared, and had to relocate to a different job in the same company, or were moved out the door, and had to seek new employment.

The production personnel whose task it was to get the product out the door in spite of the disruption and confusion around them. Your ideas, patience, and contributions are greatly appreciated.

The maintenance personnel who helped with the initial installations, and keep the equipment operational.

The finance people for their support in evaluating the proposed programs, and then followed through with such complete audits to verify the program performance.

The management personnel and executive committees, without whose support and approvals, the funds required to implement the programs would not have been made available.

The suppliers, vendors, and subcontractors who provided the technology, installation expertise and training.

To the production and support personnel who make it all work.

And finally, my many mentors, who over the years were more than patient with me and my questions. Thanks for sharing your knowledge and expertise to help make things better.

I am most grateful.

Tim Fleskes

Contents

	Page
Preface	1
1. Introduction ... What's This Book About?	3

    What This Book is About ...
    Where Do the Jobs Go?
    Productivity Growth
    Myths and Realities
    A Self-Test ...
    Problems As Opportunities
    A Guide To Manufacturing Survival

2. First Things First ... Where To Start   15

    Getting Started
    Problems As Opportunities (Again)
    Understanding Present Manufacturing Systems
    Alternative Manufacturing Systems
    Make Or Buy
    Anatomy Of a Project
    Equipment Replacement
    Quantifiable and Non-Quantifiable Issues

3. Strategies and Other Non-Quantifiable Issues   35

    What Do You Mean? ... We Can't Put a Number On It.
    Cultural and Environmental Issues
    Human Resources and Personnel
    Safety
    Quality
    Competitive Position
    Corporate Image

4. Quantifiable Issues . . . and Numbers Games   45

      What's It Worth? . . . Put a Number On It.
      Identifying And Quantifying The Variables
      Cost Evaluation And Allocation Techniques
      Operating Costs
      Fixed or Variable Costs
      Direct or Indirect Costs
      "Standard" or "Actual" Costs
      Labor and Overhead Rates
      Manufacturing Variances
      Information Sources
      Equipment Costs
      Fixture Costs
      Tooling Costs
      Labor Costs
      Material Handling Costs
      Material Costs
      Freight Costs
      Sub-Contract Costs
      Consumable Supplies
      Operational and Technical Comparative Analyses
      The Data Matrix
      Technology
      Productivity
      Thruput
      Utilization

5. Investment Considerations . . . (Capital Program)   69

      Invest? . . . You've Got To Be Kidding!
      Capital Equipment, Depreciation and Tax Credits
      Fixtures and Tooling
      Personnel Training and Development
      Financial Considerations Of Alternatives
      Discounted Cash Flow Analyses (DCF)
      Discounted Cash Flow

6. Proposals and Recommendations — 83

    Just When We Think We've Got It . . . Do It Over!
    Cover All the Bases . . . Make It Right.
    Make or Buy Considerations . . . Again . . . And Again.
    Proposal and Recommendations Documentation
    Project Format Outline
    Explanation of Project Format Outline
    Getting the Preliminary Approvals
    The Presentation . . . Are You Ready?

7. It's Decision Time . . . JUST DO IT. — 95

    Just Do It.
    The Executive Committee
    Getting Final Approval
    OK . . . But Don't Spend the Money Yet
    Implementation
    Project Implementation Schedule

8. Making It Happen . . . — 107

    Making It Happen
    Implementing the Technology
    Changing is Tough
    Final Specifications and Quotations
    Vendor Selection
    Equipment Acquisition
    Computer Support
    Operations and Maintenance Training
    System Installation
    Start-Up and Testing
    Production Run Off
    The Audit
    Typical Project Cash Flow Summary
    Cumulative Cash Flow

9. Examples and Applications 121
        Double Your Pleasure . . . Double Your Fun
        Metal Removal System
        Metal Fabrication System
        Robot Welding System
        Computer Support System

10. Finally . . . Go On From Here 145
        Finally, Go On From Here . . .

11. Not Where To Be . . . 151
        Chapter Eleven . . .

Appendices 155
        Appendix A – Summary of Charts And Graphs
        Appendix B – Axioms and Food for Thought
        Appendix C – Abbreviations, Acronyms and Definitions

Index 171
        Alphabetical By Subject With Page References

Preface

Since our country's infancy, it's unparalleled strength and power have been nurtured by two vital elements: a deeply rooted entrepreneurial spirit supported by capital commitment, and technological innovation.

Together these have provided energy to a powerful work-force and reservoir of rich human resources that have generated a manufacturing base which has established and kept America in its role as the economic and political leader of the world. These commitments have ensured our citizens the highest quality of living of any people in history, and have ensured that our children's future will be even brighter than that of their parents and grandparents. Today however, all this is more than simply challenged, it is severely jeopardized.

Even though our gross national product continues to increase slightly, the value added to gross national product from domestic manufacturing has been greatly reduced, as evidenced by the deteriorating balance of payments from a positive influence during the early 1960's, to the current trade deficit rate of over **One Hundred Billion** dollars per year!

Our domestic productivity growth rate has reduced to one third that of industrially competitive nations; to only a little over two percent annually.

The United States manufacturing base has deteriorated due to more productive foreign competition in several areas including electronics, automotive, and machine tool production.

Despite this bleak picture, there is good news. The answers to these situations are in front of us, and their potentials are rich. We can recover.

The answer is in ***UNLEASHING*** our human and technological ***PRODUCTIVITY***, and sense of commitment to once again create a manufacturing base that strengthens instead of weakens our country.

That's what this book is about . . .

1

Introduction...
What's This Book About?

A substantial part, or even all of the funds required to implement improvements in productivity, may be directly recoverable from reductions in inventories and inventory maintenance costs alone.

What This Book is About . . .

We all, especially the business owners and corporate executives should be concerned about manufacturing productivity.

How can we be convinced to make the needed strategic and financial commitments, and provide the direction required to improve our productivity and competitiveness?

Why we should . . . *"Just Do It"* . . . Or should we?

How can we identify, evaluate and implement productivity improvements in our own organizations? These potential improvements, strategies and decisions impact our business, our competition, and our future.

Over the years, management and administration of manufacturing businesses (and others as well), have been relinquished by the original owners and entrepreneurs, and given over to stockholders and executive committees. This more remote ownership and direction, along with a compulsion for short term earnings, and lack of specific manufacturing knowledge and entrepreneurial spirit, have resulted in more conservative decision making.

This overall condition and the corresponding lack of commitment of capital funds for improvements in manufacturing technology, has contributed to the deterioration of the United States manufacturing base as a whole. And, is responsible for the level of obsolete manufacturing technology being used in the United States today.

This book is about *UNLEASHING* manufacturing *PRODUCTIVITY*, and getting the United States back on track as the leading manufacturing country in the world.

It's about helping to reduce our unfavorable balance of trade.

It's about keeping jobs, even though the nature of the work will change.

We have the knowledge . . . We just need to make the commitment to *UNLEASHING PRODUCTIVITY*.

Where Do the Jobs Go?

For manufacturing companies to remain competitive, production systems must evolve, and stay current with the technologies available to get the job done.

One of the most visible issues related to improving productivity is what can happen to the jobs that are eliminated when more productive technologies and automation are implemented in manufacturing.

When robots are installed to do the work formerly performed with manual labor, what happens to the jobs?

The answer is simple . . . **They go away**.

But more importantly, what about the people? . . . What happens to them?

They may be retrained, or moved to other jobs within the company if product demand can support that decision. If not, they're out the door.

If they have the aptitude, interest, and motivation, they may be retrained into positions of maintenance, programming or other activity in support of newer technology, but many believe they are too old to learn new trades. What happens to them? For lack of alternatives, they retire.

From a very global perspective, some would say they are absorbed by the industry that builds the robots. But that is nonsense. First of all, the person whose job was taken over by a robot probably knows little or nothing about building robots. Secondly, even if they did, those jobs are already taken by younger people with the appropriate training and expertise. Besides that, most robots are built in other countries. It's a problem of displaced employment opportunities.

For example, let's assume one robot replaces two welders. (Not an unrealistic scenario in a two-shift operation, as will be seen later.) The two welders worked about 4,000 hours per year. but the robot probably took less than 40-man hours to manufacture. A bit of imbalance there, wouldn't you say? Not only that, the robots were probably manufactured overseas, most likely Europe or Japan.

But what about the alternative . . . don't install the robots. This less productive alternative is a real mistake. Continuing to add value to the product using labor intensive operations when more productive manufacturing technology is readily available, plays directly into the hands of those having access to low-cost labor. However, those willing to make the investment, (our competition) and implement the more productive technology will survive. In this case, the Jobs will move away anyway, whether we like it or not.

From a more global perspective, why is our balance of trade so unfavorable, and continues to grow worse? Failure to make the required capital commitments and implement productivity improvements contributes to our unfavorable balance of trade, and correspondingly, results directly in the migration of jobs to other areas of the world who either:

1. Have an existing supply of low-cost labor, trained to do the job, or

2. Are willing to make the long-term capital commitments to achieve higher productivity and develop their manufacturing base.

The graph on the following page "United States Foreign Trade" illustrates this significant trade deficit.

Why is our balance of trade so unfavorable?

One reason is that foreign competition Is doing a better job (being more productive) than we are at manufacturing.

There is another answer . . . **Unleash Our Productivity.**

Productivity Growth

The United States overall annual growth rate in productivity has typically been two to three percent since the early 1960's. In 1990 it fell to only two percent, the lowest in the last thirty years; half that of Western Europe; and one third that of Japan.

We must improve our productivity growth rate, or our unfavorable balance of trade will continue to worsen.

Balance of Trade

United States Foreign Trade

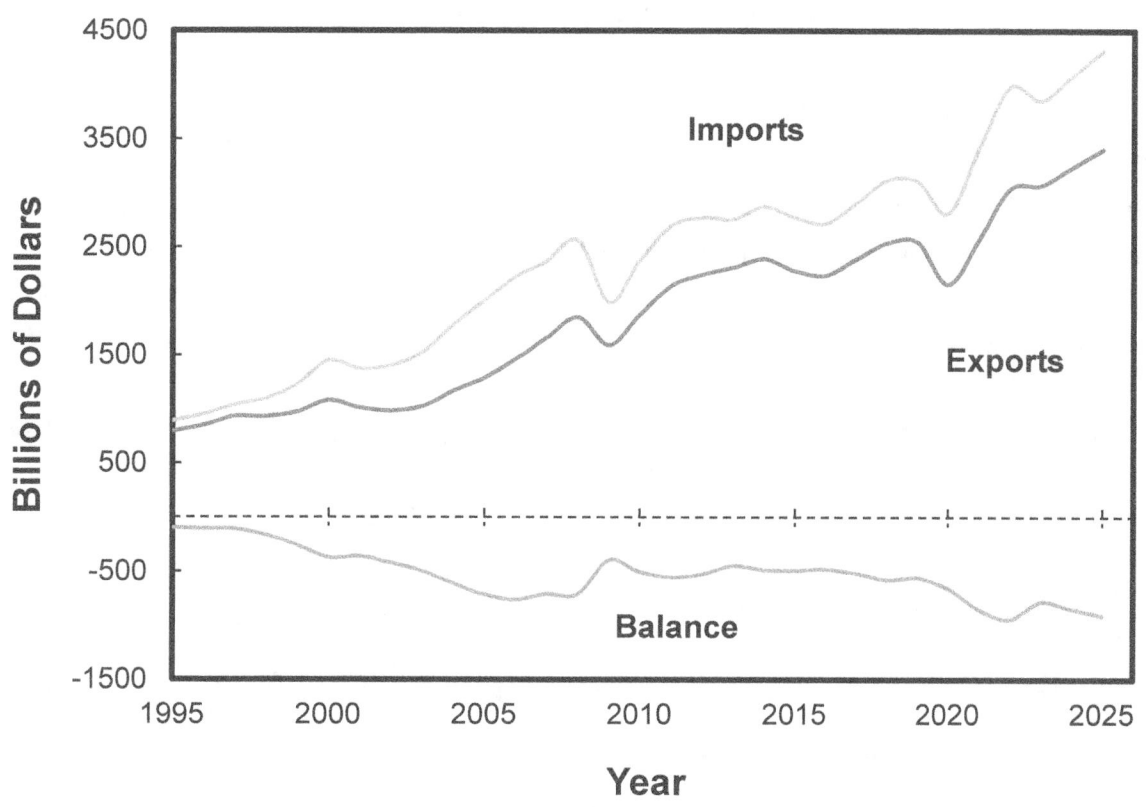

Year	Billions of Dollars		
	Exports	Imports	Balance
1995	794	891	(96)
2000	1,083	1,453	(370)
2005	1,292	2,008	(717)
2010	1,872	2,375	(503)
2015	2,281	2,772	(491)
2020	2,160	2,814	(654)
(est.) 2025	3,408	4,319	(911)

Source: World Development Indicators, 2000-2025
Foreign Trade of the United States Value in Billions. (Unadjusted)

The more unfavorable our balance of trade, the less value we (domestic labor) contribute to our own economic base. Fewer domestic jobs survive. And foreign labor is imported to maintain our standard of living.

Although the above scenario is very global in concept in principle it applies just as well locally, to an individual company or manufacturing operation. Failure to implement productivity improvement opportunities invites the competition to capture additional market share (probably ours) when they enhance their productivity, and assure their long-term position through improved market penetration. It will happen.

The fact is . . . **If We Don't Do It Our Competition Will**.

So, what is **Productivity**? . . . for now, a basic view:

Productivity is the relationship of **Thruput** to **Resources Utilized.**

Where Thruput is the quantity or amount of product generated.

And **Resources** include allowances for:

Capital	Contract Services
Labor	Materials
Supplies	Overhead

And **Time** is also a resource.

For the mathematicians:

$$\text{Productivity} = \frac{\text{Thruput}}{\text{Resources Utilized}}$$

Utilized is a very important key word here.

As will be seen later, **Effective Resource Utilization** is one of the major factors in maximizing productivity and return on investment.

The chart "Annual Productivity Growth Rate" on the opposite page clearly indicates that there is substantial room for improvement.

Annual Productivity Growth Rate

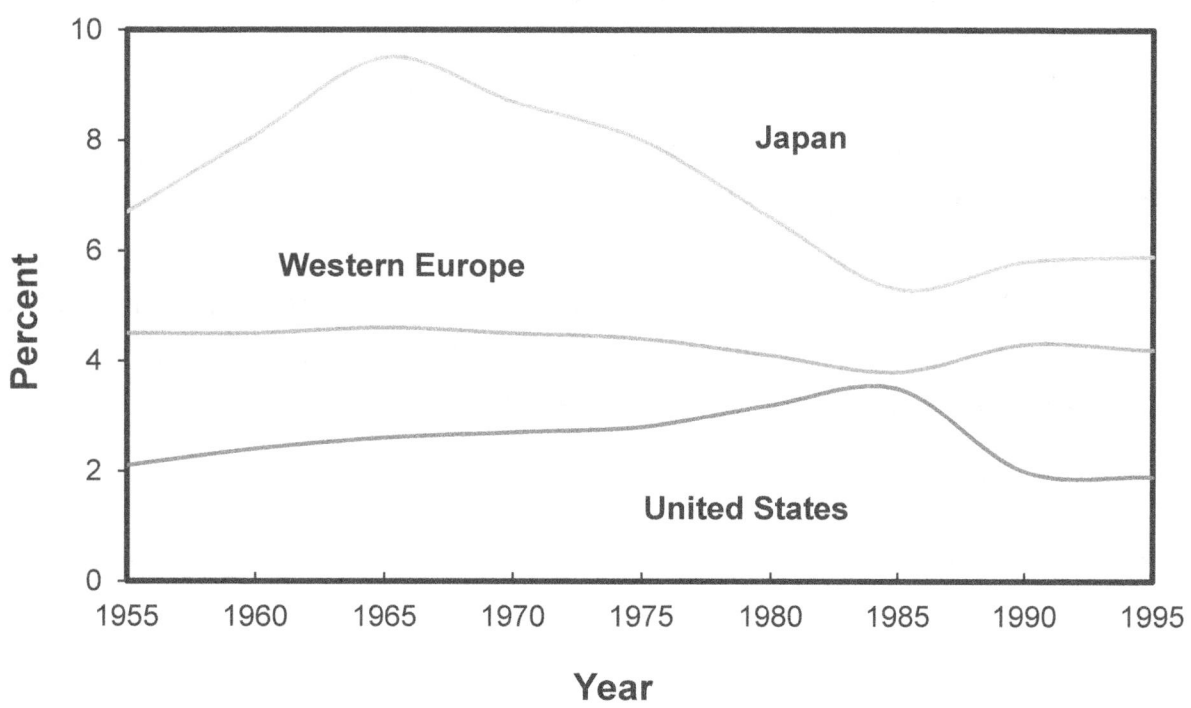

Year	United States	Japan	Germany	France	Italy	United Kingdom	Western Europe
1955	2.1	6.7	6.0	5.4	4.5	1.9	4.5
1960	2.4	8.1	5.3	5.2	5.4	2.2	4.5
1965	2.6	9.5	4.6	5.0	6.4	2.5	4.6
1970	2.7	8.7	4.3	4.7	5.7	3.3	4.5
1975	2.8	8.0	4.0	4.5	2.0	4.0	4.4
1980	3.2	6.6	3.2	4.1	4.4	4.7	4.1
1985	3.5	5.3	2.3	3.7	3.9	5.4	3.8
1990	2.0	5.8	4.5	4.6	2.8	5.1	4.3
*1995	1.9	5.9	4.6	4.5	3.0	5.2	4.2

Source: United States Department of Commerce.
United Kingdom Does not include Canada
* Estimate

Myths and Realities

Do you believe the myths? Here are a few:

<u>"You can't justify computer integrated manufacturing systems."</u>

> On the contrary. We can't afford **not** to. The support systems and information required to manufacture parts can be best maintained and managed by computer technology. We do many things better now than we used to, and one of them is keeping track of information. Think about it . . . no transcription errors, faster information availability . . . less opportunity for mistakes from manual data entry . . . etc.

<u>"Automation eliminates jobs."</u>

> If you're concerned about automation eliminating jobs, don't be. Manufacturing processes are less vulnerable to being taken over by low-cost labor when operations are capital intensive. We could coin a phrase regarding the manufacturing base:
>
> **"Don't Automate . . . Deteriorate."**
>
> We have seen enough evidence of this philosophy in action, granted, automation and more productive technology may require retraining and some displacement of personnel, but this is a far better option than not having the industry at all.

<u>"Management, labor, and government are adversaries."</u>

> We are our own worst enemy here. Whose fault is it? This is not a reason, just an **excuse**. If we are sitting on our hands, and waiting for investment tax credits, concessions from labor, or trade barriers lo solve productivity problems for us, don't. We are just not stepping up to the opportunity for

UNLEASHING PRODUCTIVITY

Let's get with it. We **can** and **must** make it happen.

A Self-Test . . .

What about my operations?
What is my Productivity Improvement Potential? (PIP)

On a scale of 1 to 5 . . .
Circle the number that best applies in your case.

Self-Test

Item	From 1	Value	To 5
Your production operations are primarily paced by:	Equipment	1 2 3 4 5	Operator
The number of people in your organization adding value to your product is:	Under 10	1 2 3 4 5	Over 100
Your product lead time is:	Acceptable	1 2 3 4 5	Too Long
Your shop equipment utilization is:	Good	1 2 3 4 5	Poor
Your set-up times are:	Acceptable	1 2 3 4 5	Too High
Your manufacturing technology is:	Current	1 2 3 4 5	Obsolete
Your shop personnel utilization is:	Good	1 2 3 4 5	Poor
Your inventories are:	Low	1 2 3 4 5	Too High
Your product costs are:	Acceptable	1 2 3 4 5	Too High
Your after-tax earnings are:	Acceptable	1 2 3 4 5	Too Low

Add the circled numbers.   My Total Score Is: _____*

If your score is 10 or greater, you are a good candidate for productivity improvement. The larger the number, the greater your potential benefit from a Productivity Improvement Program. (PIP)

* If your score is 49 or more, get some A.I., or call 911!

Problems As Opportunities

Many situations are opportunities disguised as problems. We only need to open our eyes and examine the systems and environment around us. Those who have recognized this reality **have** already started reaping benefits from implementing productivity improvement projects designed to solve "problems".

After implementing the "solutions", and experiencing the great relief and satisfaction of watching the new system at work, we always ask ourselves:

> **Why didn't we do that sooner?**

Ask the people who have made it work for them.

Unleashing Productivity

Start by establishing a long-term organizational strategy for productivity improvement. Initiate a Productivity Improvement Program, (PIP) and pick someone to administer it.

This goal needs to be specifically expressed and supported first from the highest levels, then throughout the organization, so that everyone knows they have the backing of top management **and** intermediate level managers, when they offer productivity improvement ideas.

Invite suggestions and productivity improvement ideas from within your entire organization, as well as from suppliers and vendors. Don't forget to include equipment suppliers. Be willing to evaluate the potential of all ideas received and **provide feedback** to the **source** of the idea to let them know what is being done with their idea. You will have your hands full. And, you will be pleasantly surprised at the strong strategic and economic potential represented by the collection of ideas.

When employees know that their ideas and suggestions are being fairly evaluated and considered, they will contribute their best, and everyone will benefit.

A Guide To Manufacturing Survival

Consider the deterioration of our manufacturing base in the United States. Over the years, many machine tool builders have discontinued operations because of foreign competition. And how much automotive production and electronics manufacturing have we seen move out of the country?

This migration of manufacturing to other countries has not happened only because of a few unfair economic strategies or trade regulations. We have brought much of this on ourselves through our own **compulsion for short term earnings,** and lack of commitment to improving productivity.

As we have seen, the survival of our manufacturing base is at stake.

Making It Happen . . . Just Do It.

It takes a special awareness, and significant commitment from business owners, and those responsible for administering their organizations to recover from the many years of deterioration of our manufacturing base.

The courage to make the decisions that will bring about the recovery of manufacturing in the United States is in the hands of the owners of the manufacturing businesses and organizations.

Productivity improvement ideas must be conceived, evaluated, submitted, budgeted, approved, funded, and implemented.

This is the responsibility of the owners and stockholders, (through their executive committees). They must make the right decisions.

It's a big job.

So . . . Let's Get Started.

2

First Things First . . .
Where To Start

>Involving people in change, and inviting their input and participation during the developmental and startup phases of a project will virtually assure a successful implementation of a good productivity improvement idea.

Getting Started

Now that we're convinced that productivity improvement is a real possibility in our organization. . .

Let's begin this task of **_UNLEASHING_** our own **_PRODUCTIVITY._**

We start by examining our own organization. Look around at what is happening now. After all, to get somewhere else, we have to start from where we are.

Since we are in the business of manufacturing, let's look at our processes (operations), how long it takes to do them, and the supplies needed to get our product out the door, and to the customer.

At the risk of oversimplifying, there are materials, labor, and other expenses for just being in business. There may be contract services needed for heat treating or protective coatings. Packaging supplies, warehouse and distribution costs, arid many other items too numerous to mention here, will be discussed in detail later.

The expense levels for the various components and resources required must be isolated, so that the potential for improvement in any specific area can be quantified.

There are several places to start.

A profit and loss statement and balance sheet will help identify and quantify current expenditure levels, and other required resources. (Subcontract costs and Inventory levels for example)

An asset listing showing the age and cost of capital equipment will lead to other possibilities. (Old or antique equipment will usually have no book value, and may be obsolete technology.)

A product bill of materials with cost summary is a very valuable tool. (Helps identity where the money is going for a product.)

Ask your employees or coworkers for suggestions that can lead to higher productivity. You will surely get a lot of response to that question, but be prepared.

You will probably be inundated with ideas.

Check with your vendors and suppliers. They are always willing to suggest ways for you to improve. Probably because they realize that if you improve your productivity, you will be more competitive, your market share will increase, and that will mean more business for you **and** them.

Invite someone knowledgeable about your business or industry to come in and review your operations, (maybe a consultant) and get a critique on your operations. It won't cost much, has considerable potential for results, and will definitely attract attention.

Send some of your people out into the world (for exposure), to see for themselves what is going on in your industry. Too frequently they are buried in day-to-day operations, never get away, and develop a myopic sense about the things going on around them. "They can't see the forest for the trees", so to speak.

There are many opportunities for exposure at industry trade shows and business seminars. You can spare them for a few days if you make up your mind to, and it lets them know you care about who they are, and what they think about your business. I believe they will reward this modest expense and inconvenience with a wide variety of realistic productivity improvement suggestions. (And probably some, not so realistic as well, but that's OK.)

And, of course, don't forget to include your own list of ideas.

Problems As Opportunities (Yes, Again)

Some of the most obvious sources of productivity improvement ideas are rooted in the need to solve a problem.

It is important to address productivity improvement issues from a positive perspective. More will be accomplished from this direction with less effort. Dealing with "problems". as headaches, can allow considerable negative thinking to creep into the process, and result in "patchwork" solutions. Seeing problems as opportunities establishes a more positive motivation, and platform from which productivity improvement will be the natural outcome. It helps avoid the "we've tried it before and it didn't work" excuse, whether true or not.

We must ask "how can we make it work better"? Not find reasons or excuses why it won't or can't.

Opportunities for improvement are almost unlimited. One of our jobs is to sort out the ones offering the greatest benefit the quickest and implement those first. It is important to get the Productivity Improvement Program (PIP) off the ground with some immediately visible results. This will help satisfy the people with the "short term" motivation, and give the program some very valuable initial momentum.

Even small improvements are worth the effort when they help create an environment where improvement and change are seen as positive influences on the organization, the products, and the people.

Understanding Present Manufacturing Systems

A lot goes on in a manufacturing organization. Not just the production processes, but all the support activities that are integrated into a "system" which in the end, provides the customer with the product when needed, at a competitive price.

Without understanding how manufacturing systems work, it is unrealistic to expect to develop significant gains in productivity. To get where we need to be, we **must understand** thoroughly not only **what** we are doing now but also **how it works.**

Most of the departments involved, are as follows:

Marketing and Sales	Engineering
Finance and Accounting	Purchasing
Shipping and Receiving	Production
Material Handling	Materials
Administrative	Maintenance
Quality Assurance	Personnel
Manufacturing Engineering	Vendors
MIS (Management Information Systems)	Legal

That's just about everybody!

Maintaining a positive interactive relationship among all of the above departmental functions (and even a few others not mentioned) is critical to any successful manufacturing operation.

Whenever any of these groups are potentially affected by proposed changes in the manufacturing systems, they must be involved during the planning phases of the project, given the opportunity for input into the new systems, and kept informed on the progress of the project.

Other issues that must be dealt with continually are:

> Employee Wages and Benefits
> Community Relations
> Environmental
> Safety

Adding value to materials by changing their shape or properties putting them together with other components to offer a product is what manufacturers do. It is a fascinating occupation and vocation. The challenges, when met successfully, offer very rewarding careers to all involved. Being competitive in the marketplace, and surviving (including making a profit) in manufacturing is what it's all about.

Manufacturing is **fun stuff.** Get involved and stay involved.

Alternative Manufacturing Systems

There are many ways to achieve the desired end product, probably more than we would like to count. This is especially true when looking at all the different components and operations required to get the product out the door.

Consider the requirements for a special metal bracket and fasteners that are used in the assembly of a product. They can be acquired in several ways, any of which would supply the need.

The procurement process itself is quite obvious in many instances. For example, fasteners used in the assembly of products (nuts bolts rivets) are usually provided by companies who specialize in manufacturing and suppling those products to a wide range of users. The economies of scale make it completely unrealistic for most users of fasteners to even consider making them for their own use.

Alternative Manufacturing Systems

Fasteners are considered "off the shelf" items, and unless there is something unique or special about them, it simply makes more sense to purchase that component from a vendor or supplier of those types of parts. Even if there is something special about the item, many of these companies offer support in the specialty areas as well.

On the other hand, a special or unique metal bracket is a different situation. Until this particular bracket was designed, no one had ever made anything identical to it before. There are manufacturing companies whose business is making special parts for other manufacturers. These companies, sometimes referred to as "job shops," usually (but not always) specialize, in a relatively narrow range of manufacturing technology, such as small sheet metal brackets in low or high volume.

Other companies may offer general metal removal services, heavy fabricated metal weldments, or specialize in small turned parts.

In addition, there are companies who provide specialized services such as heat treating, plating, or protective coatings (paint). These companies are more "process" oriented and usually provide only that service as one step in the overall manufacturing process.

It follows from the above, that it is entirely possible to have specialty brackets or other parts completely manufactured by vendors. Even though more than one supplier or vendor may be involved, the bracket can be completed, and brought into the company complete, and ready for use in the final assembly of the product.

So why do many manufacturers establish their own "in house" production capability for the components required by their assembly departments? There are many reasons as we shall see, among them are cost, quality, control, and response time.

The dollar investment required to manufacture specialty components economically can be substantial. In recent years, adding value in metal working technologies has become more capital intensive, and less labor intensive. This requires higher capital investment, and equipment utilization levels must be high enough to make the capital investment worthwhile. The overall end result however, (with adequate equipment utilization levels) is lower product cost, and better competitive position in the marketplace.

The **"Make Or Buy Comparison"** chart in the following section (on page 26), illustrates the cost of acquiring parts from outside sources compared with manufacturing in house, for various quantities.

Make Or Buy

So how do we answer the question: "Should we make it or buy it?"

The most obvious (and quickest) answer to the above question, when first starting out, is to outsource (farm out) the work to a supplier or vendor **qualified** to do the job. Selection of the vendor will be a function of their capabilities and capacity to meet your production schedule, and their bid price.

Clearly, there are many alternative approaches to supplying the demand for the specialty component parts and assemblies needed in manufacturing.

Some of the control criteria and variables are as follows:

Quality is Clearly the number one priority in determining vendor selection. Quantity or part volume will be the second. Then the technology involved.

Nothing gets a vendor's attention quicker than asking what their charges would be for supplying fifty to five hundred or one thousand per month of something. On the other hand, ask him about five to ten parts per month and observe the response. **Big difference** . . . they usually don't seem quite as excited about being your supplier under those circumstances. It's not worth their time, unless it will take a long time to make them.

Make Or Buy

The production technology used in the manufacturing processes, whether employed by vendors or captive (in house) operations, can be labor intensive, or capital intensive. (or somewhere in between)

Labor intensive operations, typically "stand-alone" operations, require much lower capital investment, resulting directly in more manufacturing steps and potentially higher part variability. Part quality is more difficult to control, and the part cost depends primarily on the quality and condition of the machines, wages of the employees, and the overhead, or burden application rates. It is relatively easy to set up these types of production systems because of readily available equipment, and technical knowledge. The fact that minimal capital is employed in this scenario is indicative of the vulnerability of the operation. The long-term stability of this type of operation is questionable because anyone can get into, (and out of) the business easily and quickly.

Capital intensive operations, on the other hand, require higher capital investment, but yield fewer manufacturing steps, less direct operator involvement and intervention, and quality is easier to control. These are Flexible Metal Removal or Fabrication Systems (FMS). The parts will be more consistent, and the part cost is driven primarily by the amount of capital resources required to do the job. The contribution of labor in adding value to the product is less significant because the Computer Numerically Controlled (CNC) machine tools operate with minimal manual intervention. In this scenario, one person may operate two or more machines. Unattended production systems are in sight. but whether we like It or not. they are still over the horizon a bit.

When parts are outsourced ("farmed out") to vendors, control of several significant aspects of the manufacturing process are by default given over to the supplier. these include:

Materials	Quality
Scrap Disposition	Fixtures and Tooling
Profit	The Manufacturing Process Itself
Lead Time	Price

Additionally, The material cost when purchased by the vendor, may be more expensive, because the vendor may not have the purchasing power of the end user of the product.

The revenues from the sale, use, or disposal of valuable scrap or unused material are totally controlled by the vendor.

The amount of vendor's "profit" included in the price (although justified) for the parts is unknown, and can the price quoted by the vendor be expected to remain unchanged for the long term?

Generally, (although not always) specifications and maintenance of tooling and fixtures for the job are controlled by the vendor, and may not meet appropriate standards. If you decide to move the job back "in house", or to another vendor, you may discover the tooling and fixtures, (which you paid for) may not be available, or in good condition, or both.

Response time for changes in part configuration or delivery schedules may be longer. You may not be your supplier's best customer, and when changes in delivery schedules or part configuration are needed, you could be last on his list of things to get done. Are his priorities the same as yours?

In addition to the above, the favorable cash flows generated from depreciation of capital equipment ownership benefit the supplier, not you.

If we are out of capacity, and have some "bottlenecks" holding back our shipments, outsourcing of some of those, or other operations is a definite solution to help meet market demand for our products.

If the **quality** of the component(s) in question is absolutely critical to your overall product functionality and integrity, it may be better to keep the job in house to maintain direct control of the entire manufacturing process.

If we are out of capacity, and have some "bottlenecks" holding back our shipments, "farm out" of some of those operations is a definite solution to help meet market demand for our products.

Make Or Buy

The following is a brief summary of the advantages and disadvantages for several make-versus-buy issues, from the long-term perspective of the business owner:

Make Or Buy Analysis Summary

Item	Make	Buy
Capital Investment Required	Higher	Lower
Depreciation Advantage	Yes	No
Direct Product Cost	Lower	Higher
Overhead Cost	Higher	Lower
Control of Future Expense	Better	Worse
Cost Improvement Potential	Better	Worse
Response Time	Better	Worse
Flexibility and Control	Better	Worse

The **"Make Or Buy Comparison"** chart on the next page illustrates the approximate relative total cost associated with the **"outsourcing"** of metal removal or fabrication work, compared to **"in house"** manufacturing, at various volume levels for **four** different manufacturing technology scenarios.

	FMS Technology	**Stand-Alone Technology**
In House	Scenario A	Scenario B
Out Source	Scenario C	Scenario D

As the chart (Lines A through D) illustrates, if overall product demand, or volume is high, there may be considerable cost advantage to outsourcing the work, even though it is expensive, because in house equipment utilization would also be high. Also, major capital expenditures can be more easily justified economically, and the corresponding family of benefits will follow.

Make Or Buy Comparison (Year 2025)

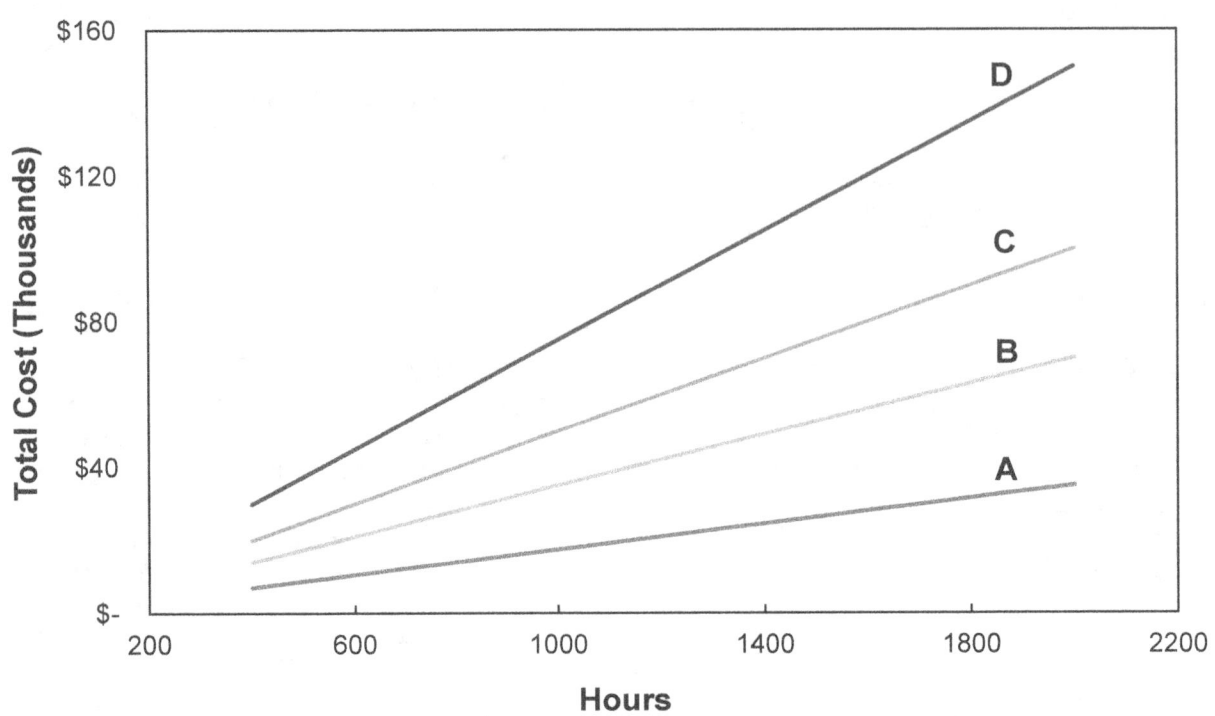

	Total Cost of Procurement			
	In House		Out Source	
	FMS	Stand Alone	FMS	Stand Alone
Machine Hours	**Scenario A**	**Scenario B**	**Scenario C**	**Scenario D**
400	7,000	14,000	20,000	30,000
800	14,000	28,000	40,000	60,000
1200	21,000	42,000	60,000	90,000
1600	28,000	56,000	80,000	120,000
2000	35,000	70,000	100,000	150,000
Additional Parameters				
Cost per Machine Hour	$17.50	$35.00	$50.00	$75.00
Labor Cost per Operator per Hour	$35.00	$35.00	$75.00	$75.00
Number of Setups per Year	1	6	1	6
Inventory Turns Per Year	50	6	50	6
Operator to Machine Ratio	1 to 2	1 to 1	1 to 2	1 to 1

Anatomy Of a Project

The following discussion takes us through the various phases of a productivity improvement project. The chart on page 31 outlines the process, from concept to reality.

The first step in any project is to identify the opportunity.

Get an Idea.

A preliminary program description will outline the present operational processes related to the program, then describe the concept of how that might be changed, and what the benefits of the new program or operating scenario are expected to be. This concept outline should include the estimated costs of implementing the new program, summarize the strategic and economic advantages, and indicate how long it would take to implement the new system.

The source, or the originator of the idea should be recognized, and a letter or copy of the preliminary concept proposal should be sent to the originator, acknowledging and thanking them for their contribution. A note of appreciation, or other recognition, from those in high places wouldn't hurt either.

The potential program is then submitted, (hopefully along with many others), to the people in the organization responsible for evaluating and budgeting funds for capital improvements. The potential projects are reviewed and, if the program is accepted, included in the capital budget. This does not mean the project has been approved. There's still a lot of work to do, but if it is really a hot idea, it can jump to the top of the list in a hurry. and perhaps even bump or replace a project with lesser potential. It could also be rejected outright at this stage for reasons that should be documented. If this is the case, the originator should be notified, and an explanation provided.

Capital budgeting in manufacturing organizations is an ongoing task where a moving long term (five year?) capital plan is developed. The greatest attention is given to the front end of the five-year plan but the long-term plan assures some level of continuity from both budgetary and technological perspectives.

Sometimes, if a project has really significant potential and promises powerful returns, it might bypass the budgeting phase entirely, go directly to the more detailed cost/benefit stage, and proceed rapidly from there to the head of the line. This might happen if new technology becomes available that was unanticipated, or competitive strategy requires immediate implementation of new, or different production systems.

Generally, the time required to implement a productivity improvement idea, depending on the complexity and need, can take anywhere from five weeks to five years to implement. This may be surprising, but it's true. Most of the time, if programs are approved for the budget, (depending on funds availability, and overall capital budgeting), and if the project is confirmed as viable from the more detailed evaluation analysis that follows, they will proceed at a relatively rapid pace.

The cost/benefit analysis phase examines the project in considerable detail to shake out the bugs in the program and develop a solid proposal. This very detailed analysis includes investigations into potential alternatives to the basic idea, contingencies, technical evaluations, materials and work force implications, A detailed financial analysis, including a Discounted Cash Flow (DCF) projection is done. The project schedule and equipment specifications are developed, (involve the potential users of the equipment and get their valuable input into the potential system configuration) and formal quotations from suppliers are received and evaluated. Technical comparisons of competitive equipment offerings are performed. Other non-quantifiable issues such as safety and environmental are examined for impact.

It is critical to the success of the program that the evaluation is done thoroughly and accurately, and that all potential questions anticipated, and open issues resolved. Preliminary approvals should be in place from the key groups and individuals in the organization that will be impacted by the program. Production managers finance people, and other support personnel should not only "buy off" on the concept, but also the final proposal, so that one idea is being submitted for approval. The options must have been thoroughly examined, and the correct option selected. Keep high level executives advised of the specific strengths of the program, so that there are no surprises at the executive level when they review the program for final approval.

Anatomy Of a Project

The final proposal and recommendation should contain **no surprises**.

The formal documents required for the release of funds, and personnel adjustments if needed, should be prepared and submitted along with the proposal, so that all high-level business, and the required signatures can be taken care of at one time. Cover all the bases.

Remember:

Surprises Are Bad . . . No Surprise Is Good.

Get on an executive committee meeting agenda for program review and formal approval. The formal presentation of the project to the decision body can occur any time. These are busy people. Be ready to present the proposal at their convenience. When presenting the project, be prepared, be honest and be right. Answer all questions, and ask for approval. Does this sound like a sales pitch? It is.

Four things can happen at the final review:

1. The project is approved as outlined.

2. The project is tabled, to be resubmitted at a later date. Sometimes this is done to delay the program because of insufficient short-term cash flow to support the program.

3. The project is rejected as outlined and sent back for changes and re-evaluation. If this happens, we didn't do our job thoroughly.

4. The project is rejected outright. This should be a very rare occurrence, but if it happens, we probably should have known in advance, and not submitted the program the first place.

Assuming the program is approved, now the work begins.

The implementation phase of the program begins with finalization of the system specifications, and equipment acquisition. The people who will be using the equipment should be involved again during this phase of the operation, not only to take advantage of their knowledgeable contribution, but because their involvement will help solidify their commitment to making the new system work the way it should.

After the equipment is on order, the final implementation schedule can be established, and training and support systems development can proceed.

When the equipment arrives, it is installed, started up, and de-bugged. The equipment suppliers should be heavily involved in this process.

The equipment operators and maintenance people are brought up to speed on the new system. The new equipment starts producing product, and the system and product quality are verified. Thruput comes up to expected levels, and the system is released to production.

The new system is now "on line".

After a run-in period designed to thoroughly shake down the system, the learning curve is behind us, all the "bugs" are fixed, and the system has been operating successfully for some period of time (a month or two), it's time for the auditors. Their job is to do a formal financial evaluation of the system. They will verify that program expenditures are in line and within budget limits, and that the new system is functioning as expected.

Be available to provide the auditors with any help they may request in identifying specific technical features or other information about the system.

If we did our job correctly, we probably won't hear from the auditors again, but if we screwed up, we must be ready to explain the discrepancies.

If all has gone well, we carve another good notch in our credibility belt.

The diagram on the opposite page shows the anatomy of a project.

Anatomy Of A Project

Project Anatomy

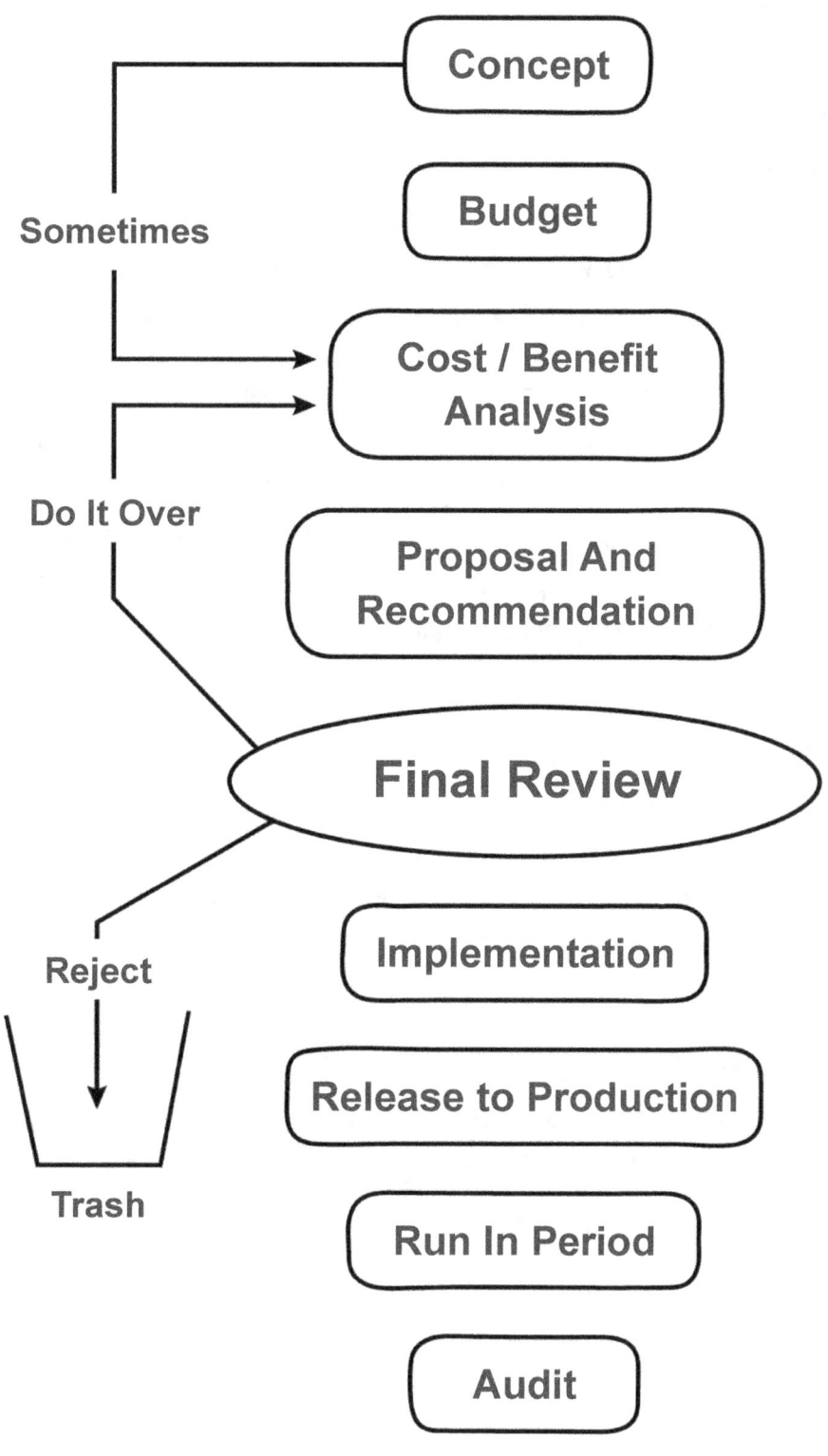

Equipment Replacement

When (or whether or not) to replace existing equipment is a question that arises continually in industry. But the question should also be asked: "Should we just get rid of this equipment?" The control criteria for this decision takes many forms.

The main question to ask (and answer) is: "How much is this equipment being used now?" If it is not absolutely essential, and being used very little, or not at all, get rid of it. It is taking up valuable space, we have to clean around it, and there is always a tendency to put a body in front of it to make it seem needed.

If the equipment is being used, and is an essential part of the manufacturing operations, then it deserves appropriate consideration and attention. If maintenance is excessive, or quality difficult to control, these are usually evidence that the machine is wearing out, and needs rebuild, upgrade, or replacement. Remember, responsibility for equipment maintenance and replacement is implied when the decision is made to install the technology in the first place.

Sometimes rather than just "rebuild", it makes sense to "upgrade" the existing equipment. If the equipment is very specialized in nature, or very expensive, this alternative is quite viable, and should be seriously considered. This could include a complete mechanical rebuild along with new control technology. And might also include integration of newer, more productive processes at the same time.

If newer, more productive technology is available, and cannot be included in the rebuild or upgrade of existing equipment, then replacement with new, or more advanced used equipment may be the more appropriate decision.

The financial implications of equipment replacement, although they may be substantial and must be considered, may not be of primary concern at this time. It could be more of a strategic question: "Do we want, or need to continue this capability in house?"

After evaluating the alternatives, including the relevant financial and strategic implications, decide what to do, and just do it.

Quantifiable and Non-Quantifiable Issues

How do we place a value on things like strategy, capital, quality, labor, depreciation, overhead, inventories, other expenses, equipment utilization, and thruput when they are involved in a productivity improvement project?

The answer is . . . **very carefully**

Many of the above items (and many more that are not itemized above) are very difficult, or impossible to quantify, but some are relatively easy.

The important idea here, is to admit that some things cannot be quantified, and some can. In the chapters that follow, each of these subjects, and their strategic and economic implications, will be discussed individually in more detail.

It makes no sense to spend a lot of time analyzing and quantifying the economic impact of a variable when the magnitude of that variable is minute with respect to the overall program.

On the other hand, it is foolish to ignore variables whose strategic advantages may be significant, but are difficult or impossible to quantify.

But, more on these issues later . . .

3

Strategies and Other Non-Quantifiable Issues

Be kind to Manufacturing Engineers.

What Do You Mean? . . . We Can't Put a Number On It.

Strategic and other non-quantifiable issues that impact the capital investment decision process are frequently dismissed as unimportant, or ignored because they are difficult or impossible to quantify.

The price paid for ignoring non-quantifiable issues can be crippling or even fatal to a productivity improvement proposal, and can adversely affect the business for not only the short term, but also the long haul.

If, for example, the competitive advantage of a potential production system with shorter lead time to delivery, or greater flexibility is not acknowledged, and the project is killed, or shelved, the competition not only can, but probably will, implement the same or similar systems.

Then they will possess that competitive edge in the marketplace.

It can be argued that shorter lead time, or flexibility can be quantified. But, the numbers associated with these variables are very speculative at best, and can not only render the financial analysis and economics associated with the proposals less credible, but also drag the evaluation phase out while appropriate numbers are being agreed upon.

It's better to admit that it's best not to quantify them, and get on with the project than to get bogged down in differences of opinion over what they are worth.

For example, identify the potential benefit of shorter lead time as a strategic advantage, and let the decision makers in high places interpret, and place a value on those benefits in their own terms. The worth of increased market share potential coming from shorter lead time, or greater flexibility is best evaluated by people with broader knowledge of the market. The benefits from shorter lead times, for example, will probably be viewed in terms of increased revenue potential, or a competitive advantage resulting directly in increased sales.

A series of strategic advantages, or maybe just one, can make the difference, and tip the balance in the decision process in favor of a productivity improvement idea.

At the same time, it is just as important to identify the potential negative impact or non-quantifiable variables to keep the proposal balanced and objective. (There is not much room for prejudice in any proposal.)

From a strategic perspective, is it better or worse than what is being done now?

Like the optometrist asks, "Is it better this way, or that?"

Make the decision.

Cultural and Environmental Issues

Air and water quality, noise, energy consumption, movement of materials through a local area (material flow), scrap and waste products disposal, and resource utilization and recycling, are some of the local environmental issues challenging manufacturing systems today.

The people and things around us are affected by what we do, or don't do in manufacturing. The increased traffic caused by higher concentrations of employees from a new facility in an area can have serious effects on a community. The potential negative aspects of these changes may be offset by more jobs and better economic stability for the local area, but when it is done with full consideration for those directly affected, the best results will be forthcoming.

Our Government has seen fit to remind us of our responsibilities in these areas by establishing at the Federal level the Environmental Protection Agency (EPA), and the Department of Environmental Quality, (DEQ), and their Local counterparts to establish standards and local guidelines for air, water, and other emissions affecting our environment.

Consideration for cultural and environmental issues must be an integral part of any productivity improvement Program (PIP) proposal. Change is difficult, but we must evolve if growth and prosperity are to continue. Whatever we decide to do, or not do. . . **we affect those around us**.

Human Resources and Personnel

How do people feel about their jobs, and their company? (yes, "their" company). Whether they "own" it or not, they adopt it as their own. It is "their" job at the plant. Employees want and need to be proud of the facility and the products they make there. Their sense of pride in who they are is at least partly rooted in their sense of contribution and satisfaction at work. The entire health of a community can be derived from the image of the businesses there.

If the company is busy, so is the community.

If the company is proud, so is the community.

If the company is challenged, so is the community.

An individual's pride in their work comes from their capacity for doing it well. If they have the latest and best tools and equipment, they know no one can be better at what they do than they can. More than that, they know no one can be more competitive at building their products than they are. There is no fear of foreign competition here. They have the tools to get the job done and they do it.

Quality is apparent everywhere.

And, oh yes, a living wage, (possibly even a profit share incentive), and the confidence that their jobs will be there tomorrow, are the things that successful companies are made of.

What more personal inspiration and motivation is needed for.

"UNLEASHING PRODUCTIVITY"

Safety

Consideration for the health and well-being of all employees in an organization is primary.

Even though the Occupational Safety and Health Act of 1970 (OSHA) requires a safe and healthy work environment, manufacturing has been, and continues to be committed to this objective and willingly accepts this responsibility.

Any productivity improvement project **must** fully consider the safety implications for not only the equipment operators, but people who may be in the surrounding area as well, such as supervisors, visitors, or maintenance personnel.

Involving the operators, maintenance, and safety personnel in the configuration and installation of the safety systems will help assure a fully functional system, and just as importantly, one that is understood by all concerned.

The funds requested for any productivity improvement program **must** provide for the purchase and installation of the required safety equipment. This may be in the form of fences, guards, floor mats, or electronic curtains, that automatically prevent machine motion and/or potential injury, when personnel access areas or zones of the manufacturing system where machine components are in motion, or can move automatically.

Some redundancy is appropriate here. This is very important.

The safety systems required to prevent access to potentially hazardous areas or "zones" of the equipment, must be included and installed during the installation phase of the project.

Safety is not a negotiable issue.

Quality

How much is quality worth? (It's priceless!)

What is your business worth?

Without **quality**, the business . . . **will not survive.**

Learn this well:

>**Quality = Survival**

Evidences of failure to provide quality in manufacturing are numerous.

Two major examples are, the quality problems of post-World War II Japan, and later with our own automotive industry. Both of which, I'm sure, we are all quite familiar.

Regarding marginal quality: **Simply do not allow it.**

But, let's bring this concept home to our own local situation. The things we can touch, the things that are real to us, and the things we can do something about.

Quality can be interpreted as meeting specifications. But it goes far beyond that.

Remember, the customer's perception of quality is not just numbers and specifications. It involves the overall performance of the product and the integrity of the business. It is a feeling . . . a confidence that is projected by an organization, when they meet delivery commitments, and respond and service the needs of their customers in a timely way.

The business not only provides the product, it also provides the support service and network to the user that tells the customer that the business is there for the long haul.

The principles of quality and integrity must be imposed throughout the organization, (especially on productivity improvement projects), to produce quality products.

It follows then, that the support systems, equipment, and the operators, in order to produce "quality" products, must possess their own integrity to assure continued product thruput to the required specifications.

Quality assurance (inspection) fixtures and gauges can play a significant role in verifying compliance with product specifications, and reduce greatly the amount of time required to confirm product integrity.

The essential point is that it is the manufacturing system that produces the product, and only with appropriate inspection and other Statistical Process Capability (SPC) systems in place, compliance with specifications, and quality products will be assured.

But, remember this:

No quality "control" system ever made a bad part good.

It is just not possible to inspect quality into a product. And it doesn't help a whole lot, to find out after the fact, that bad parts were produced.

Making bad parts is a terrible and inexcusable waste of time, materials, energy, effort, and capital resources.

Therein lies the case for Statistical Process Capability (SPC) systems.

Competitive Position

The overall market for our products, although shared with our competition, and changing somewhat from year to year in volume and configuration is relatively fixed.

Unless influenced by other forces, such as research and development breakthroughs, competition, or increased demand due to changes in product applications or utility, it is unlikely that the overall (global) market will change very much.

But, we can affect our market share.

The natural rule of "**survival of the fittest**" hits very close to home in manufacturing, and there are many aspects of production systems that can, and do influence the demand for our particular products within the global marketplace.

Price notwithstanding, product features, flexibility, and availability are among the more important qualities asked for, and needed by the customer. Adapting rapidly to changing customer needs has become essential to survival.

Manufacturing systems can and are being developed and configured to provide those qualities, thereby giving a "**competitive edge**" to the businesses with those systems in place.

Any time productivity improvement ideas are examined, these features should also be considered as part of the proposal to enhance the ability of the organization to respond to customer needs. Usually, lower inventories, better material flow, and faster lead times will result as well.

Combining manufacturing operations, eliminating manual intervention, integrating supplier involvement into the manufacturing systems, and other more productive schemes will in fact improve your position in the marketplace, and give you the competitive edge.

Remember this:

If you don't do it . . . your competition will.

What is increased market share worth to you?

Your survival may be at stake.

Corporate Image

The image you project to your customer, and the community at large is important.

How would you feel, as a customer, or as a member of the community, to be brought into a manufacturing organization where the production systems are archaic, and maintaining quality is a struggle every step of the way? I suspect your confidence in this organization would be shaken. As a customer, you would probably spend at least some of your time wondering where you could get your work done by a more productive company.

As a member of the community you would probably just wonder . . .

Your image as a manufacturer goes far beyond the product itself. It includes your sense of commitment to manufacturing, to your customers, your people, and your community.

Are you, as a manufacturer . . . **"Being all you can be?"**

Your customer wants, and needs to know that his supplier is using the latest and best technology to produce products for him. This is how you help your customer to be as competitive as possible.

He is **"Being all he can be"** and you're helping him!

He can brag to his customers about the technology you, as his supplier, are using in the production of his parts.

The community is very proud to have such a distinguished and progressive manufacturer as yourself in the neighborhood.

And your employees are convinced that you are doing everything in your power to stay in business, and keep their jobs in the neighborhood.

4

Quantifiable Issues . . . and Numbers Games

Effective utilization of resources is the key to achieving acceptable return on investment, and optimizing payback period.

Not Minimizing Investment.

What's It Worth? . . . Put a Number On It.

We begin by placing a dollar value on the variables associated with productivity improvement ideas. And later, evaluate the economic impact of what we're doing now, compared with the alternatives.

A full range of applications, from relatively small expenditure requests for small tools that help make a job easier, to capital improvements involving major capital equipment expenditures, including computer support systems, will be discussed.

And the rules will apply to everything in between as well.

To begin with, all costs and benefits are expressed in today's dollars. No attempt is made to adjust the value of a benefit or expense with respect to time, for inflation or potential increases in the cost of labor, materials, or supplies, until the Discounted Cash Flow Summary (DCF) phase of the project.

The Discounted Cash Flow (DCF) model will compensate for the time value of money and inflation at the project summary stage. But more about that later.

Remember, the more accurate our information, the better the projections will be as well, and the name of the game is . . . **credibility**.

We **must** do our work now, so we don't have to do it over again later.

Identifying and Quantifying the Variables

Placing a monetary (dollar) value on a variable, first involves defining that variable. For example, what is the cost of labor? We could jump on a number, (say $20.00 per hour) but without defining what we mean by "labor" we don't stand a chance of selling the number upstairs to an executive board trying to decide whether to buy a new machine. Since the number we use will significantly impact the economic analysis of the project, we'd better know what we're talking about.

Cost Evaluation And Allocation

For example, let's consider labor. Should the cost of employees' vacations, medical benefits, and sick leave be included in the *cost* of labor? What about supervision? The answers are yes, yes, and yes. These are some of the issues that must be quantified in order to place a *dollar* value on the variable called "labor".

What about the cost of materials, transportation, supplies, and other expenses? Similar detailed analyses are required before numbers for these variables can be established with the required integrity and credibility.

What about "overhead" or "burden", as some cost accountants like to call it. And, what do we do with depreciation?

It's a lot of work . . . so let's get on with it.

Cost Evaluation and Allocation Techniques

When examining the "cost" of something, it is important to isolate the dollars, and identify what is actually being accomplished with the expenditure. For example, if we paid $50.00 per hundred pounds for steel plate, does that price include freight in? Was that price a one-time price, or do we typically pay more or less depending on availability and lead time? Where is the Freight On Board (FOB) point? And how many pounds were actually spent in the manufacture of the product in question? Was any scrap left over? Was it sold? For how much? How many parts were actually produced using the material, and how many were scrapped? (yield) When the bill was paid, was it discounted for early payment? How much?

Too many questions you say . . . you're right. But it's better to answer them now, because if you don't, you'll wish you had.

In order to establish the economic and functional credibility of an analysis, these questions **must** be answered. Take the questions out of the issues before they have a chance to come back to bite us. And if we don't, be assured, they will. As surely as bears live in the woods, they will. I guarantee it.

Detail, detail, and more detail. Complete, accurate, and thorough analyses establish credibility. That does not mean that all this detail will be forwarded in the final proposal package. It most certainly will not. The final proposal, as we shall see later, will be very brief and to the point.

What does go with the proposal is the confidence and belief that it was done correctly, thoroughly, and accurately.

Operating Costs

Operating costs are, as you might suspect, just that. There's nothing complicated about them. Things like raw materials (steel), supplies (industrial gas, or wire used for welding), and rent, just about anything that would show up on a Profit and Loss Statement (P&L) are considered operating costs.

When evaluating a productivity improvement idea, it is important to identify all of the operating expenses that would be impacted or change if the new system were put in place. Some expenses may increase, while others may decrease, or be eliminated entirely.

To get a complete and comprehensive idea of what is involved, the present manufacturing system must be thoroughly understood and evaluated.

> **Complete understanding of the present manufacturing process is essential in order to proceed effectively with the analysis. Implementing any productivity improvement project requires that the manufacturing processes evolve from where they are now, to where we want them to be.**

Hopefully implementation will, or under some circumstances must, happen without any interruption in product flow or thruput.

The main idea is that the costs that will change as a result of installing the new technology must be identified, and quantified.

Now, on with what we mean by "cost" . . .

Fixed or Variable Costs

Fixed costs are expenses which typically do not fluctuate when production volumes are changed. Usually, small incremental changes in production rates do not require corresponding changes in the fixed expense level for the business operation. An example would be rent on the building where the manufacturing operations are performed. The product thruput could be increased or decreased by ten or twenty percent without affecting the monthly rent on the building. If production levels are increased or decreased by ten percent, the number of supervisory employees probably would not change either.

On the other hand, if producing each product requires one hour of labor, this would be considered a variable cost, because each additional product made would require additional labor. The materials required to produce the product would also be considered a variable cost.

Fixed or variable costs may be either direct or indirect costs.

Direct or Indirect Costs

Direct costs are those which can be attributed and allocated directly to the product, whether expensed or not. Sometimes, when expenditures are difficult to directly allocate to the product, they are "expensed". This means their cost is recovered through the "overhead" or "burden" cost allocation rates within the standard costing system. Direct or indirect costs, if they can be allocated directly to the production of the product, should be isolated and included as line items in the detailed economic and financial analyses of the project.

Indirect costs, conversely, are all other costs that are not direct, and cannot be allocated directly to the production processes. Things like janitorial services, the water bill, and the accounting department are considered indirect costs. These are normally "expensed".

Direct costs can be either fixed or variable.

Are you confused yet? . . . Cost Accounting 101 is next.

"Standard" or "Actual" Costs

If your organization has a standard costing system, the numbers established (standards) are primarily designed to recover operating costs over a period of time. There are many other uses for standard costs such as inventory valuation, performance reporting, and manufacturing variances, but these will not be addressed at this time.

Standard costs include allowances for direct labor, depreciation and other overhead, and tend to average the cost of labor and other components of cost. The values may include a mark-up on materials to recover freight costs or scrap allowances, and even some amortization of tooling or fixtures.

One of the main components of "standard costs" are "standard" times, or the amount of time (in minutes or hours) that it is expected to take to produce the product. This "time" is then multiplied by a "standard" rate in dollars per hour or minute, called a "labor and overhead rate" (see next page) to help generate an expected, or target, product cost.

> **"Standard" costs should not be used to evaluate the economic and financial benefits of a Productivity Improvement Project.**

Because of averaging, and other elements frequently included in the "standards", they will not reflect accurately or appropriately, the actual potential changes in cash flows within and outside of the organization for a specific Productivity Improvement Project.

In order to establish the "actual" costs related to a project or application, it is necessary to remove (as much as possible) the influence of averaging inherent in standard cost systems. Averages tend to compromise (muddy-up) the actual cost picture. It is very important to develop numbers that directly relate to the application, and quantify specifically their impact on the organization. To properly evaluate a Productivity Improvement Project, the actual direct costs must be identified, quantified, and allocated appropriately.

Labor and Overhead Rates

The labor and overhead (sometimes referred to as burden) rates are dollar values per hour, or minute, set at a level designed to recover the direct labor costs, and overhead (burden) or indirect expenses. They are used in conjunction with standard times, and other costs such as materials, to set the standard costs for the products. The rates are reviewed and adjusted periodically to values that will consistently recover operating expenses.

Values for inventories, and product costs are established using these rates, and they are used as a base for monitoring actual costs.

Manufacturing Variances

Since actual costs and manufacturing times will vary throughout the year, the actual costs and times are compared regularly with the standards to see how things are going. Actual material costs are compared with material cost standards to generate purchase variances, and actual labor times (usually from work order summaries) are compared with the standard labor times to generate labor variances. Labor variance reports may be generated as frequently as weekly or daily.

Variance reports are reviewed regularly to evaluate the impact of actual costs on the business operations, and serious discrepancies are examined and reconciled immediately.

The dollar values of the variances may be booked monthly as adjustments to expenses, so that the income statement (P&L), and balance sheet will reflect as close to actual conditions as possible.

Information Sources

Where to go to find really solid information about the actual present cost of doing something depends on the kinds of cost accounting support available.

The best place to go to find out what you are paying for materials, or supplies is the accounts payable group. You could ask purchasing, and they will cooperate by telling you what they think they are paying. Most of the time they will be pretty close, but they probably won't mention much about the discount schedules they've negotiated for early payment of invoices, or the times they've had to authorize premiums to get the materials by the required delivery date. The actual invoices paid over a period of time will give the best information about what the materials or supplies are actually costing. Check to see if the invoices are being paid in time to deduct the discounts (if allowed) for early payment.

Labor is more difficult to isolate. Work order histories probably give the best indication of how much labor is or has been charged into the product. But even here, this information should be confirmed by observation of actual shop operations if possible. What it really takes to get the job done, and how much time is actually being charged into the job, may be quite different. These variables need to be isolated and the data verified before we can have the required confidence in the numbers that come to the surface. Besides, the process of investigating the operations enhances our understanding of the manufacturing processes, and further establishes credibility for the analysis.

Another way of verifying the data is to monitor the actual thruput over a period of time, and count the people required to get the job done. When the numbers from different sources agree, you can believe you are close to the right answer.

Finally (one more check), ask the people doing the work and the foreman or supervisor how long it takes to do the job. They will usually give you credible numbers.

And, if you're still not sure . . . go through the analysis again.

Equipment Costs

The most significant cost associated with productivity improvement programs is usually the cost of new or replacement equipment and related facilities. Expenditures for machine tools, and robots which account for this major outlay of funds, can amount to hundreds of thousands of dollars, and easily run into the millions.

Usually, the equipment technology is flexible in nature so that even if the product configuration changes, the technology is still applicable, and the benefits of the system will continue to accrue. For example, a robotic welding system doesn't care (within limits) what the weldments look like. It has the capability to weld regardless of the product configuration.

Be very careful when the equipment configuration is closely dependent on the product configuration. Product obsolescence can be a cruel reality. If a production system is built to satisfy a specific product configuration, and that product is discontinued, you may find yourself with a whole bunch of very expensive unusable iron on your hands.

The potential capital equipment expenditure really gets the attention of the finance people in an organization for obvious reasons. Where are the funds going to come from to pay the bill for the equipment? Even if the payback period is fairly short for the project, somebody has to provide the funds up front. The negative cash flows on the front end of the project must be managed, but once the equipment is operational, the benefits and more favorable cash flows that follow will help pay the bills.

The equipment may be purchased outright using existing funds, leased, bought on contract, or financed by the bank. In any case, it's the responsibility of the finance group to work it out. It helps a lot if the organization is functioning from a positive cash flow position, has a strong order board, and lots of orders on hand.

Many equipment suppliers require funds in advance of delivery, especially if the equipment is somewhat specialized. Some money with the purchase order, and "progress" payments, may be required. The payment schedules can vary, and are negotiable, especially at the time the actual order is placed.

A common scenario might be: thirty percent with the order, thirty percent during the construction phase, thirty percent on completion of the equipment at the factory, prior to shipment, and the remaining ten percent thirty days after installation and start-up.

Even though a delivery schedule and commitment has been agreed upon, the progress payments if required, should be dependent as much as possible on clearly definable stages of the project, not the calendar, so that we can see where the money is going, and progress toward completion can be verified.

For example, the first payment of 30% could include the cost of any special engineering required for the equipment or process. This should be completed prior to release of funds for the second progress payment. The second payment of 30% could cover the cost of materials and major components for the equipment. The third payment of funds 30% could occur when the equipment is operational, "run-off" on the suppliers floor, and released for shipment. The final payment of 10% should be held until 30 days after the equipment is installed and operational on your floor. Unfortunately, sometimes this last payment is used as leverage to help "encourage" the supplier to fully comply with all specifications.

> **Note: The equipment and component warranties should not start until after the system is operational on your floor.**

The equipment cost can be written into the project analysis in several ways. First, it will show up in the capital expenditure summary as a lump sum amount, as part of the overall project costs. Second, the equipment depreciation will be written into the cash-flow analysis, to reflect the corresponding tax advantage. The write-off period for capital equipment for tax purposes is controlled by federal tax regulations. If investment tax credits are applicable, they are included as well. A third way of including the expenditure in an analysis is to distribute or allocate the equipment costs over the project or equipment life, thus directly reflecting the expected utilization levels of the equipment.

Other amortization schedules may be established for the equipment, depending on the overall objective, such as setting a rate to apply to the use of the equipment internally, or how much to charge a customer for the use of the equipment.

Fixture Costs

Fixtures are devices built to hold the work piece(s) **rigidly** in a predetermined specific orientation or position, allowing work to be performed on the material such as machining, or metal removal operations as may be required on a casting.

Another example would be an assembly or welding fixture for a particular group of parts to be assembled or welded together. This type of fixture would locate and hold the various parts in their appropriate respective positions to facilitate the welding or assembly operations.

Several fixtures may be required for any particular job.

Remember these things about fixtures:

> **Fixtures cannot make bad parts good.**

And fixtures . . .

> **Cannot make good assemblies from bad parts.**

And . . .

> **Bad fixtures cannot make good products.**

Fixtures are also designed and built to facilitate inspection operations and procedures, verify compliance with specifications, and confirm product quality.

Fixtures can be general purpose in nature and be used over a wide range of product configurations, or be highly product specific.

Usually, fixtures are designed and built for specific product or part configurations. For this reason, they are typically written off over a much shorter term than equipment. This is because the product life in its present form may be limited. Product obsolescence may also be the culprit here. If the design is relatively fixed and can be predicted to have long term stability, then longer write-off periods for fixtures may be appropriate if consistent with the life of the fixture.

Tooling Costs

Tooling is where the work gets done. It is the drill bit used in the machine that makes the hole, or the punch and die used in the press to blank or form the shape. These are the devices that change the shape or configuration of the material, and this is when the value is added to the material.

Tooling can be configured to minimize the need for checking the parts to verify compliance with specifications. For example, a die set that punches an entire four-hole pattern at the same time can greatly reduce or eliminate the need for checking the distance between the holes, since the hole spacing and position is already defined by the tool configuration and does not change. If the holes are punched individually, the distances between the holes must frequently be checked to verify compliance with specifications.

Initial tooling costs can be significant, and tools **will** require maintenance. Drill bits for example will not make holes forever, must be sharpened regularly, and replaced when worn out or broken.

Be kind to your tools and they will be kind to you.

Tooling can be general purpose in nature such as drill bits, milling cutters, or press brake dies. Or they may be very product specific, like form tools used in turning operations, broaches for a specific internal hole configuration, or a punch and die set for a specific part design or hole pattern.

Tools costing less than $2,000 each are usually considered supplies and are therefore "expensed" or written off as soon as purchased.

However, if the tools are expensive (costing over $2,000), they will usually be "capitalized" and maintained on the books as an asset.

Inventories for both expensed and capitalized tools are typically maintained and monitored as a means of managing expenditures and controlling the utilization and cost of tools.

Labor Costs

The cost of labor over the years has been, and continues to be a significant component in the cost of manufactured products. But this is changing. More and more of the value added to the product is being done by machines requiring very little operator intervention. Even so, the equipment operator is still a very essential part of the production process. It is not possible (yet) to run most production systems without equipment operators.

So how do we place a value on the contribution of the operator to the product? It was easy when each machine required an operator, but that's not true anymore. One operator can operate or manage several machines. And not only that, the machines are highly flexible, and can be working on several different products, at the same time. This tends to create a cost accounting nightmare. We used to have the operator tell us what he was working on by clocking in and out on work orders, and this information was used to help place a value on the product. It just can't be done that way anymore, because operators and equipment are so versatile. Should we turn all of our equipment operators into cost accountants? **Absolutely not.** If we did, there wouldn't be anyone left to operate the equipment and get the product out the door.

The cost of labor should be factored into the product or process based on the amount of time the person spends tending to the demands of that particular part or operation. The appropriate allocation can easily be determined by analysis, and if performance is a concern, monitor the thruput or products completed regularly as needed.

Remember this:

> **It is the combined contribution of the man, the machine, the computer, the fixture, and the tooling that get the job done. Breakdown of any of these components including the data required by the computer, results directly in the temporary failure of the production system.**

Material Handling Costs

When the materials involved in the manufacturing processes are bulky or heavy, material handling costs can be significant. These costs are usually "expensed" and recovered through overhead or burden rates. This is done because they are difficult to allocate to specific product configurations, and in most organizations, do not typically represent a large portion of the overall operating costs.

However, a particular productivity improvement project may impact how the materials are handled in an organization, not only because they might be handled differently, but also because they may be handled at different times. Newer production systems strive to reduce production lead times and improve the material flow, thereby impacting the existing material handling systems.

These potential variables must be appropriately considered and quantified in the project analysis.

Material Costs

The value of the raw materials used in the production processes are of course included in the product cost. Establishing the amount of material required for the product can be quite involved. The raw material must be brought on site, then processed into the configuration required by the product. Usually, not all of the material is used in the process, some parts produced will not be shippable because they were used in set-up operations, or scrapped because of quality constraints. Quality problems are known to occur in manufacturing from time to time, and a certain amount of material purchased for the job will be discarded or unused, either in the form of remnants, or scrap. Depending on the manufacturing processes employed, the amount of material actually needed to make the product can be quite different from what we may expect. Problems with a particular part of the manufacturing process can reduce good part yield significantly. We must watch for, and reflect these conditions in the project analysis. Be aware that these things can and do happen.

Material Costs

For example, a formed sheet metal bracket may require an irregularly shaped blank to be produced prior to the forming operation. The bracket, if made from sheared material, may require a rectangular blank. But if the shape of the blank lends itself to material "nesting", considerably less raw material may be required for a given quantity of parts. If the blanks are produced using a flame cutting process such as laser, plasma, or oxygen-fuel cutting systems. It is the net "yield" in finished parts made from a given amount of material that will establish the actual material requirement, and in turn, the cost.

If the raw material is in the form of a casting, the yield of good finished machined parts may be a few less than the number of castings started due to porosity, or parts used in set-up operations, which were not suitable to complete. Most of the time these castings are returned to the casting supplier for credit, but the credit would only apply to the ones not finished due to casting imperfections or porosity. And even though that's what should happen, it doesn't always.

In addition, remnants or scrap can usually be sold to a recycling company. For purposes of the project analysis, the revenues generated from this sale should be credited back to the cost of the parts. In most routine cost accounting systems this allocation is almost impossible to achieve, and the revenues from the sale of scrap are simply treated as "other" income. If costing the parts on a project basis, this allocation **is** necessary and expected, and can be handled quite easily.

The end result of all this work, is a fairly accurate representation of the material cost in the product, which would qualify as an "actual" material cost for purposes of the project analysis.

Purchased parts used in assemblies are also considered as "materials". Establishing the "actual" cost of these items in the product is very straightforward. The purchase orders, vendors invoices, and accounts payable vouchers provide excellent sources for this information.

Freight Costs

The costs of transporting materials when contracted to a commercial carrier are quite easy to track. The price charged for their services is shown on the freight bill, and can be picked up directly. If on the other hand transportation of the material is handled "in house", the costs are much more difficult to establish. It is clear that if changes in the production systems result entirely in the elimination of in-house transportation systems, the commercial cost of getting the job done will directly offset the reduced in-house expense levels. Evaluating these alternatives is very difficult, and one can only estimate the cost of handling transportation of goods as an in-house operation. Fortunately, these expenses are usually not significant in the overall scenario, and can be estimated for project purposes quite effectively.

Sub-Contract Costs

The value for work done by subcontractors, such as heat treating or finishing operations, can be established quite easily from the contractor's invoicing for services. But, **pay special attention to who provides for the transportation of the goods,** this will certainly impact the value placed on the service.

Consumable Supplies

The cost of consumable supplies such as welding wire, industrial gases, cleaning solvents, adhesives, sealants, etc., can be determined from supplier invoices, then applied to the amount of those supplies required by the product.

All of the above variables should be considered when trying to establish an "actual" cost for a product or process. If the magnitude of the variable is very small with respect to the overall analysis or, if it can be determined that there is no difference in that variable for the proposed systems versus the present, they may be omitted from the analysis on that basis. But you can be assured, someone will ask about them.

Operational and Technical Comparative Analyses

Gathering all of the relevant information, and organizing it in ways that make sense is very important. When people inquire about the project they frequently ask "Why is the proposed system better?" It's a big help to be able to illustrate the relevant variables in comprehensive ways that show how it is being done now, compared with the planned or proposed systems.

With the personal computers and software available these days, it is quite easy to show relevant information in many different ways. Spreadsheets are one of the most powerful tools that can be used for this purpose. Word processors, database and project scheduling applications are also very useable tools.

Outlining all of the project variables on a spreadsheet, along with their relative impact on the present system and proposed alternatives, creates a very informative and comprehensive data summary.

The Data Matrix

The data matrix is a very flexible tool, that can grow to almost any size, and include virtually all fixed and variable aspects of a project. They are especially useful when used to develop cost, savings, and utilization projections for different demand scenarios.

The information in a data matrix doesn't have to be all numbers. Using qualitative statements, such as poor, good, better, or best, are also effective ways of illustrating the relative advantages or disadvantages of alternative systems. Ask yourself the question "what would I like to know about this project?" then answer the questions in the matrix.

Presentation tools such as graphs, slides, and handouts are easily prepared from the data, and save a lot of time. The data matrix is like a picture, and we all know, "a picture is worth a thousand words."

Some data matrix applications are dedicated to specific tasks such as the Discounted Cash Flow analyses (DCF). This is because the data handling algorithms can be nasty and are probably best left to specialists experienced in handling that type of information.

A somewhat limited example of a technical data matrix comparing three alternatives, horizontal machining centers is on the facing page.

While some of the information is very specific, other data is more general. For example, the machine weight shown in the data matrix reflects the estimated installed weight of the three different machines. It is quite general in nature, but at the same time gives an indication of the mass of the equipment. Some analysts believe that greater mass in a machine tool is better because it tends to reduce machine vibration and results in better long term mechanical stability.

An example of more specific information would be the axis speeds. The relative rapid traverse rates of the three different machines, (based on the belief that faster is better), would lead some analysts to favor the "A" or "C" alternative.

There is a procedure for giving the different variables different levels of importance called "multi-attribute" modeling. These procedures are somewhat involved, but do provide a method of quantifying each variable, and weighting them for importance so that an alternative can be selected just by adding the numbers. Sometimes this procedure is used as a tie-breaking tool when a consensus solution cannot be reached.

Remember that what is most important to some people, may not be important to someone else, and they all may have a voice in the decision.

Keep in mind that a data matrix is only one of the tools used in a project analysis. It is only part of the whole picture.

Even after all of this, the final choice will probably be a judgement call. But, at least it will be an informed one.

Data Matrix

(For Horizontal Machining Centers)

Item	Units	A	B	C
Manufacturer		Domestic	European	Japanese
Model Number		630	24/35	24/30
Machine Weight	Pounds	35,000	40,000	37,400
Pallet Capacity	Pounds	3,000	3,000	2,646
Size	Inches	24.8 x 24.8	24 x 24	24.8 x 24.8
Accuracy	Inches	±.0002	±.0002	±.0002
Work Envelope				
Diameter	Inches	35.4	40.0	41.3
Height	Inches	37.4	36.0	37.4
Axis Travel				
"X" (Length)	Inches	40.0	40.0	39.4
"Y" (Height)	Inches	31.5	30.0	31.5
"Z" (Depth)	Inches	31.5	30.0	29.5
Rotary Table	Deg/Step	1	1	1
Axis Speeds				
"X" (Horizontal)	In/Min.	940	400	945
"Y" (Vertical)	In/Min.	940	400	945
"Z" (Spindle)	In/Min.	940	400	787
Spindle Data				
Maximum Speed	RPM	7,000	4,000	6,000
Maximum Torque	Ft-Pound	530	600	766
Horsepower	HP	30	35	30
Tool Changer				
Number Of Tools	Quantity	80/120/180	40/80/120	40/80/120
Tool Length (Max)	Inches	17.7	18.0	19.7
Tool Weight (Max)	Pounds	66.0	50.0	59.4
Tool Change Time	Seconds	3.5	8.0	6.5
Lead Time	Months	6	8	7
Price Per Machine	Dollars	$425,000	$550,000	$450,000

Technology

Examining the specific technologies being offered that have the potential of satisfying your application is a difficult task. Obviously, use of the data matrix technique will prove very helpful in evaluating the possible alternatives. Most equipment builders provide brochures, and other detailed technical information about their systems as part of the equipment quotation. There may be gaps in this data, from supplier to supplier, depending on the attributes of their equipment that they are particularly proud of. Suppliers have a tendency to promote and talk most about the aspects of their systems that are superior to their competition. But, if asked, they will usually provide other information, especially if they are interested in getting the order for the equipment.

> **The equipment suppliers will, (as is to be expected), expound on the positive aspects of their system. But don't hesitate to ask for, and get the information necessary to compare directly with their competition.**

From the information provided in their quotations, a very complete and comprehensive attribute list can be developed, along with specific values that relate to those attributes. It is safe to believe that if the information is important enough for them to publish, it is probably important to you.

As seen in the data matrix from the previous page, some of the attributes for evaluating a machining center would include machine axes rapid traverse rates, work piece envelope, tool change time, machine accuracy, and spindle horsepower, torque and maximum speeds. An individual supplier, if they are not particularly proud of their offering for a specific attribute, may be reluctant to provide the information, but have them supply the data anyway. It will make them more aware of what information is being required in the marketplace, and what their customers are concerned about.

The information provided in the quotations should be considered proprietary, and should not be specifically made available to competitors. That does not mean that the potential suppliers shouldn't be made aware of their shortcomings, and challenged to improve their systems so that better technical solutions will be available in the future.

Productivity

The relationship between thruput or the amount of product produced, and the resources utilized to get the job done is the best measure of productivity. Getting more product from the same amount of material, or using less material to get the required thruput is being more productive. The same principle applies to other resources as well, such as time, money, labor, supplies, contract services, equipment, and overhead.

Improving productivity is getting more done with less.

But, do not use higher productivity as an excuse for generating bigger inventories. The cost is too great.

In general:

If you're not going to ship it, don't build it.

There are some exceptions to the above, but they should be individually analyzed, and maximum inventory levels carefully established.

One of the most important aspects of equipment analysis is evaluating the productivity that can be expected from the system. There are several ways to establish a value for the productivity of a machine or production system. Productivity is sometimes expressed in terms of parts per hour, or minute, but just as important is the "uptime" that can be expected from the equipment, or the amount of other resources needed to operate the system. These directly affect the capacity of the system for thruput. For example, it doesn't help very much to be able to produce parts at the rate of fifty per minute, if the machine will stay running only half of the time.

Talking with other users and owners of similar or identical equipment, supplied by the same vendor can reveal very important information about how well the system can be expected to hold up for the long haul. Talk with the maintenance people who take care of the equipment and are responsible for keeping it operational, and the equipment operators. These are the best sources of information about what you can expect from a production system.

Thruput

The production system, as alluded to above, may have an impressive production rate, but what is completed and ready to ship each day is what it's all about. That's **thruput**. This is what generates the revenue for the organization. This is what pays the bills.

> **Thruput is product out the door.**

Do not play games with Thruput.

> **It is either there or it isn't.**
> **If it isn't, down you go.**
> **Simple as that.**

Thruput is about the difference between reality and theory.

This book started out with a definition of productivity expressed in terms of thruput and resources utilized, not production rates. Believing in thruput as the measure of effectiveness of a production system separates the realists from the theorists. The theorists are good at speculating, (and we probably need some of those around), but it's the realists that get the products out the door, that generate the revenues, that pay the bills.

Getting the product out the door (thruput) requires a manufacturing system that coordinates resources with product demand. How well we do that is the measure of the productivity (getting more done with less) of our organization.

Our very survival depends on getting that job done efficiently.

And doing it better than our competition.

We must deliver the product that meets specifications, when needed, where needed, and at a competitive price. That's the bottom line.

Utilization

Manpower, equipment and other resource utilization levels are key elements in determining productivity. Only by utilizing the resources needed for production effectively can the rates and expense levels associated with the application of those resources be reduced, and therefore minimize the projected product cost.

Improved raw material utilization is another significant area for potential productivity improvement. For example, just the application of "nesting" the work pieces in metal fabrication can easily result in ten to twenty-five percent reduction in material requirements, and therefore cost in the product. (Nesting is the process of arranging the material blanks in a sheet of material that minimizes waste.)

Sometimes, minor modifications in the design or engineering of the product can result directly in much improved levels of material or other resource utilization.

The economic and financial aspects of equipment justification are linked directly to the planned utilization levels of the resources. Both fixed and variable expenses must be allocated based on anticipated resource utilization levels.

The forecast levels of equipment utilization in the project analysis must be related directly to anticipated product demand, not the capacity of the system. Just because a system has the capacity to produce one thousand widgets per year doesn't mean it should. The quantity that are actually produced should be a function of product demand.

Underutilization of equipment is probably the single biggest reason why forecast return on investment and payback periods are unacceptable, and projects rejected. But, that is the reality of the matter, and if the forecast utilization levels, based on demand, cannot generate the required return on investment and payback, then so be it.

Obviously, products should not be produced just to keep the equipment busy. This will simply result in bigger inventories, and that just doesn't make sense.

5

Investment Considerations . . . (Capital Program)

Eliminating opportunities for manual intervention in the production cycle will result in significant reductions in product costs, and improve quality and thruput.

Invest?... You've Got To Be Kidding!

Capital improvement programs are a very necessary and continuing effort on the part of industry designed to maintain or improve the productivity of the manufacturing systems. The initial commitment by the original owners and entrepreneurs to invest in an idea, carried with it the commitment to maintain and sustain that system once it is in place as well. But the responsibility for maintaining the manufacturing base these days lies with the current owners. There are many examples of situations, where the assets of the organization were literally stripped and then left to disintegrate, along with the jobs. Therein lies one of the causes for the deterioration of the manufacturing base in the United States.

> **Lack of long-term commitment.**

Capital programs designed to maintain and improve the long-term manufacturing productivity of the organization must be provided in the long-term financial planning budgets. Funds are provided in the budgets for research and development to assure that the product has a firm long-term position. Similar commitments to provide for capital improvements must be included as well, to assure the long-term stability, and financial viability of the manufacturing systems.

For some folks, the idea of investing in their own well-being is difficult to comprehend. They figure that once they've spent the money, and the assets are in place, their commitment is over and they need not worry about it again.

> **Wrong, Wrong, Wrong.**

The capital assets of the organization need long-term attention and maintenance too, just as much as the operations side of the business.

> **Capital budgeting and planning must be part of the long-term operating strategy of the organization.**

But let's be realistic as well. The expectations of reasonable financial benefits and other returns, come along with making the commitment to invest.

> **This is completely reasonable and justified.**

The question is . . .

What's a reasonable return?

And how do we calculate it?

To most people, after-tax profit is the return they are seeking from their investment. But this is not entirely where it's at. Just because a company shows relatively low after-tax profits doesn't necessarily mean they're not making money. Let's look at after-tax earnings. These are the dollars that are added to the coffers at the end of the accounting period, and made available by the owners or executive committees for payment of dividends, or reinvestment in the organization.

Capital Equipment, Depreciation and Tax Credits

Along with investments in capital equipment, come allowances for depreciation. This allowance directly reduces the tax liability of the organization. The depreciation schedules and amounts are controlled by federal tax regulations, and may or may not be related to the useful life of the equipment.

The bottom line here is that the **depreciation** amount **is not a cash out expense**, and it directly reduces the level of taxable income.

Some would say the funds accrued from depreciation are set aside for equipment replacement, and in a very global sense this is true.

But in fact . . .

> **The funds go into the bank and can be used for any business purpose, including payment of dividends.**

Investment tax credits (historically ten percent of capital investment) also increase earnings, not only by reducing taxable income, but by directly reducing the tax liability. From time to time our federal government has seen fit to selectively turn these on or off, depending on the administration, the current economic projections, or their ability to convince congress that it's a good idea at the time. As of this writing, they are turned off. Sometimes tax credits can be passed along to sister companies in the organization or carried forward to a subsequent year. If a company is not paying any taxes, an investment tax credit does them little good.

The calculations reflecting the above-mentioned depreciation and investment tax credit benefits are provided for in the Discounted Cash Flow (DCF) analysis model used in projecting the potential Return On Investment (ROI), Payback period (PBP), and Net Present Value (NPV) of a project.

Facilities

Capital expenditures for facilities such as buildings or land, although almost always included in major capital improvement programs involving new site development, are not usually needed as part of most productivity improvement projects, because most improvements are implemented within an existing facility. New equipment can usually be installed within the space occupied by the old existing equipment, and probably will not require any additional support services such as electrical power, or compressed air, since these are probably already in place.

The overall space required for installation of new equipment and systems may even require much less room than the systems they are replacing, but additional space may be needed temporarily to help facilitate the transition.

Keep in mind however, that if additional land or building area is needed for the project, and must be acquired, then those costs must be included in the project analysis.

Fixtures and Tooling

The funds required for fixtures and tooling are just as important as the equipment itself. They are like links in a chain. If not provided with sufficient integrity, the system will break down, and the program will not achieve its objectives. Even though the amount of money required for fixtures and tooling is typically a smaller part of the overall investment, the importance is nevertheless significant, and must **not** be minimized.

Fixtures hold the work piece, while the tooling is used to change the shape or configuration the product. The fixture can be product specific, or general purpose in nature. If the fixture is product specific, its useful life is directly related to the life of the product, or job, and therefore the risks from obsolescence are greater. However, if the fixture or parts of it, are general purpose in nature, then there is significant potential for a much greater useful life. Most of the time the fixture and tool requirements are a combination of the above. This makes it more difficult to specifically allocate the fixture and tool expense.

Generally, fixtures and tooling are written off over relatively short periods of time, thereby reducing the risk of financial loss due to obsolescence or other influences. The fact is however, that once the funds are expended, they are history, "sunk" so to speak, and life goes on whether that specific job continues or not.

It is important to recognize that the depreciation schedule established for tax accounting purposes probably has little to do with the actual useful life of the equipment, fixtures or tooling. The write-off period allowed for tax purposes is usually more favorable, in the sense that the asset can be written off (depreciated) over a shorter period than the real useful life of the hardware. And, since depreciation is a non-cash-out expense, an amortization or allocation schedule related to the projected useful life of the hardware is much more useful as a means of allocating, or recovering the costs of hardware.

> **In short, depreciation should be omitted from the expense schedule and replaced with an allocation or amortization plan when operating expense projections are made.**

And, if the projections are being used to justify the expenditure, the depreciation or amortization should be omitted entirely from the benefit calculations.

Computer Support

The computer support required for manufacturing systems can vary all the way from none to a full-blown dynamic computer support environment, such as might be required by a computer integrated manufacturing system (CIM). Computer support systems consist primarily of hardware and software, and within those categories, a broad spectrum of options are available, ranging from personal computer (PC) based systems to main frame applications.

The computer-support systems are typically used for programming, scheduling, tool maintenance, thruput reporting for cost allocation, information management, data communications, and other applications.

> **The important consideration here is to require that the computer systems support the manufacturing operations, not the other way around.**

Believe it or not, there is a strong tendency for some computer support and management information systems (MIS) groups to believe the equipment should support the computers.

> **We must not forget why we are here.**

This is not meant to take away from the valuable contribution the MIS groups make to the overall functionality of manufacturing systems, it simply means that the overall objectives of product thruput and customer support must come first.

It is sometimes tempting for the group generating the support software to want the manufacturing system to support the computer requirements, but we must not forget why we're here. It's the manufacturing systems that add the value to the product and generate the revenue, and it's the role of the computer systems to support that objective.

From an overall perspective, the manufacturing and information systems groups must work together to achieve the objectives, and whatever each can do for the other to make their jobs easier, is what should be done.

The capital and maintenance costs of the required computer support systems must of course be included in the productivity improvement proposals, and generally the quicker they can be written off, the better. Computer technology is changing so rapidly, that systems put in place today, will be outdated in just a few years. This doesn't mean they won't work for the long term, but it does mean they may become difficult to maintain because the components used in the computers may no longer be available, and operating systems will have been upgraded to faster and more powerful systems.

Personnel Training and Development

Manufacturing technologies are changing rapidly, and it is difficult to keep pace with the new concepts and ideas utilized in new equipment.

> **The needs of personnel training and development is obvious and absolutely essential.**

Machine and equipment controls, for example are undergoing the same kind of evolution as the computer industry. Equipment requirements for better accuracy and faster thruput have forced the development of more advanced, faster, and more user-friendly equipment controllers. New generations of machine controls and programmable logic controllers (PLC's) are being released about every two years.

Along with these new controls comes the need for knowledgeable equipment operators and maintenance personnel, who must understand how the equipment works, and so are forced to become computer literate. This does not, and will not happen by osmosis, even though some people responsible for training budgets act like that is the case.

> **The need for computer literacy has become apparent in almost all facets of our culture.**
>
> **Industry and educators must accept their responsibilities as teachers and trainers.**
>
> **And, employees must accept their responsibility as learners.**

Training costs money, but it pays off. The funds must be provided, whether as part of productivity improvement programs, or as part of a continuing and ongoing effort within the organization to upgrade the knowledge base of its personnel.

Put some computer-literate younger employees together with some of the not-so-computer-literate older employees, and let them learn from each other. Both have a lot to offer, and both have a lot to learn.

Many opportunities for specific and relevant training are available through equipment builders and educational institutions.

Most large companies provide educational incentives for executives and other personnel attending community colleges and university programs. This should be extended to include all levels of personnel, even to the point of remedial reading if needed. We, as a culture, can only benefit from education, and the benefits to industry are automatic.

Financial Considerations of Alternatives

When considering a production system upgrade or improvement, several viable alternatives will probably present themselves as possible ways of getting the job done. An implementation cost can be established for each, along with their corresponding economic and strategic benefits. These alternatives can then be evaluated side by side so that the advantages and disadvantages of each will become readily apparent.

The data matrix format conveniently isolates the major and minor financial and strategic differences between the alternatives. Two or three of the alternatives which adequately represent the range of viable choices will surface and should be included in the final proposal.

Select the most viable alternatives from the above choices and use these in the final recommendation and proposal. It is important that the choices not only reflect the full range of viable alternatives, but also be limited to a few final choices, (two or three at the most). This approach allows the people evaluating the recommendation and proposals at the executive level to readily understand the proposals and absorb the relevant strategic and cost-benefit differences.

> **Too much information, or too many choices presented at the final stage can easily bog down the project.**

Too many potential choices tend to raise many more questions, make the whole evaluation process more complicated than it needs to be, and will lead the executive group to wonder why the people offering the proposal or recommendation can't decide what they want to do.

> **The executive committee or decision body is looking for clear alternative recommendations of what should be done.**

Although they are definitely interested in, and want to understand what is being proposed, their responsibility is to select from proposals with major strategic and financial differences. Don't try to snow them with too many facts and numbers. This will backfire, and all alternatives will be rejected until a clear, or limited set of recommendations are identified and presented.

Discounted Cash Flow Analyses (DCF)

The Discounted Cash Flow (DCF) analysis model is a financial tool used to assist in quantifying the financial aspects associated with capital investments with respect to time. Its primary contribution is the calculation of Return on Investment (ROI) and Payback Period (PBP), along with the Net Present Value (NPV), for a project, given a specific set of conditions.

Used in combination with other analyses and summaries, it is a valuable tool in establishing the relative financial worth of projects, and the incremental return on investment, when several alternative proposals are being considered at the same time.

The discounted cash flow model examines and summarizes impact of the various cash flows associated with a project with respect to time. It includes not only the initial program cost, but also the impact of direct savings, depreciation, investment tax credits (if applicable), expected changes in inventory levels, taxes, and the residual value of equipment (if any). The present values for the future cash flows are generated and summarized as present dollars, and the key investment ratios are developed.

The financial criteria threshold for accepting or rejecting projects probably already exist for the business organization. These are known as "hurdle rates". A typical set of numbers for a general-purpose project might be:

After Tax Return On Investment	15%
Payback Period	3 to 4 Years
Net Present Value	10% of Program Cost

Projects that are product specific, which have a greater risk due to potential for obsolescence, will usually require better numbers.

The discounted cash flow analysis also provides insight into the potential impact of the proposed program on the profit and loss (P&L) statement and balance sheet for the organization.

A basic example of a five-year Discounted Cash Flow (DCF) summary is on the following page.

Discounted Cash Flow Summary
(Basic Example)

Item Description	Time Now	Year 1	Year 2	Year 3	Year 4	Year 5
Program Costs						
Equipment	$750,000					
Fixtures	150,000					
Expenses	100,000					
Total:	$1,000,000					
Cash Flows						
Depreciation		$199,500	$306,000	$177,000	$112,500	$105,000
Reduced Inventories		25,000	10,000			
Residual Value of Equipment						150,000
Annual Savings		150,000	250,000	250,000	250,000	250,000
Taxes	38%	57,000	95,000	95,000	95,000	152,000
Tax Credit*	10%	N/A				
After Tax Earnings						
Future Values		$317,500	$471,000	$332,000	$267,500	$353,000
Discount Rate Per Year		5.0%				
Present Values		$302,382	$427,213	$286,797	$220,076	$276,589
Program Summary (After Tax)						
Net Present Value		$513,057				
Internal Rate of Return		16.7%				
Payback Period (Years)		3.2				

Note: Assume for this example that the equipment was sold at the end of the fifth year for its residual value, and the income from that sale is therefore taxable.

*Investment tax credits are not currently active.

Potential income from the sale of equipment that is replaced or eliminated, and the residual value of the equipment after the project term should also be considered in the discounted cash flow analysis.

Avoiding potential future expenditures for equipment replacement, and extensive maintenance of existing equipment can also be included as offsets to the overall cost of the program since these potential expenditures would not be incurred if the program is approved.

Preliminary discounted cash flow analyses should be developed for several proposal alternatives so that their financial viability and potential can be evaluated and monitored from the beginning of the project.

Since the organization has probably already set acceptable ranges or hurdle rates for payback, return on investment, and net present value, project proposals should not be submitted to the executive groups which will not meet those pre-established internal criteria for acceptable investment opportunities, unless specifically requested to do so. This will happen from time to time if it is clear that very significant strategic benefits can be anticipated from a specific program.

The discounted cash flow analysis model provides the opportunity to check the financial sensitivity of the proposed programs, and enables the project proposals to be tuned to show the various financial ratios resulting from different levels of equipment utilization, product thruput, and capacity utilization. It also gives the people proposing the project a preliminary view of whether the program will be approved from a financial perspective.

Keep in mind however, that even if the financial numbers are somewhat marginal, strongly favorable (non-quantifiable) strategic benefits and implications of a project can override marginal financial numbers, and the project can be approved on the strength of significant potential strategic advantage.

The following is a checklist of monetary items that should be considered in the discounted cash flow analysis summary:

Cash Flow Summary Checklist

Program Costs
- Land
- Buildings
- Equipment
- Freight In for Equipment
- Equipment Installation
- Facilities Modifications
- Personnel Training
- Computer Support
- Fixtures
- Tooling

Offsets to Program Costs
- Depreciation
- Inventory Reductions
- Future Capital Cost Avoidance
- Residual Values of Equipment
- Income from Sale of Assets

Changes In Revenue
- Increased Sales
- Potential Improved Market Share

Changes In Expenses (Savings)
- Cost of Materials
- Cost Of Supplies
- Sub Contract Costs
- Cost of Direct Labor
- Material Handling Savings
- Inventory Carrying Costs
- Maintenance Savings
- Freight Savings

There are probably others as well, but the above items cover most of the monetary issues that can directly impact the discounted cash flow analysis of a program. Keep in mind that the items that change significantly as a result of implementation of the project are the ones that will determine outcome of the analysis.

6

Proposals and Recommendations

Personal and informational credibility and integrity must never be compromised. Making a successful proposal is entirely dependent on doing what you say you will do when you say you will do it. Always keep appropriate parties advised of significant and relevant open issues related to the project, especially events which may delay the schedule.

Just When We Think We've Got It . . . Do It Over!

After all the preparation, analysis, and documentation, and we think we are ready, the project still must be reviewed.

> **Does it make sense?**
> **Look it over one more time.**

Sometimes we get so involved in the details of the program, we can't see the forest for the trees. Step back and take another look. You'll be surprised at what you might find.

Overlooking the obvious can be **fatal** to a project proposal. Have you ever bought a machine that wouldn't fit through the door, or built a boat too large to get out of the shop?

> **Surprises are bad news.**

Often a third party, with no ax to grind, can quickly review and bring to light things that we should have thought of but didn't. It's definitely worth the check, and you will go a long way to establishing real credibility for your proposals.

Cover All the Bases . . . Make It Right.

It feels good to present a proposal, knowing that there is little or no chance of being surprised with questions we haven't already thought about and addressed. There is no substitute for being right the first time. As the saying goes, "You never get a second chance to make a good first impression."

> **You may not get a second chance to**
> **submit the project for approval.**

Your **Credibility** . . . **Credibility** . . . **Credibility** is at stake.

No, I don't stutter. This is really important.

Make or Buy Considerations . . . Again . . . And Again.

This question is perpetual, and valid. Think of solid answers to this alternative, and be prepared to show the relevant strategies, cash flows, equipment capacities and utilization levels to support your position.

> **The facts are the best reasons in the world for doing what needs to be done.**

Some people believe that facts are negotiable, but be careful, this is very slippery logic. One set of "facts" can blow another set of "facts" right out of the water.

For example, the fact may be that the vendor's price is less, but it also may be true that the price is only good for one year. So what happens after that?

> **Tell the whole story.**

Discuss issues such as quality, lead time, flexibility, customer response, and corporate image. Many, or a few, intangible and non-quantifiable issues can (and do) swing decisions at the board level in favor of the project, even though the economic and financial issues may not be as strong as we would like them to be.

Proposal and Recommendations Documentation

The formal proposal is the written summary for the project, and must be complete, but kept short and concise. It will definitely be read and examined by knowledgeable people, and must be absolutely accurate and truthful in every respect.

How much information to include in the final proposal is a good question. Everything that is available on the subject should definitely **not** be included. Enough data should be included to enable the reader to completely and accurately understand the main strategic, technical, and economic issues that are relevant to the project, and reach at least a tentative conclusion regarding the program.

Obviously, the amount of information provided with the final proposal can vary substantially, depending on who the proposal is prepared for, and their perceived needs. It is better to include something in the summary that someone important believes is needed, than leave it out, even if you think it could be omitted.

Charts, spreadsheets, and graphic representations of concepts are especially useful because they show a clear picture of entire concepts and relationships at one time, and are quick and easy to understand. The graphics should be supported with brief explanations of their relevant key points within the text of the proposal.

> **The decision makers really are busy people and can't necessarily take the time to wade through lengthy and boring volumes of information.**

And remember . . .

> **If you leave something really important out, it can kill the project. Especially, if it is specifically important to any of the key decision-makers, whether they are on the board or not.**

The Project Format Outline on the following page shows an arrangement, and the kind of information which should be included in a project proposal.

Pick out the relevant data, and go for it.

Project Format Outline

1. **Program Title or Name:**
   Total Dollar Amount:
   Reference Number:

2. **Synopsis/Summary:**   There is a better way.
   Give a brief explanation of the project.

3. **Problem/Opportunity Statement:**
   Background Information:
   Age of equipment, obsolete technology, excessive maintenance costs, having trouble maintaining quality.

   Present System Definition:
   Describe how the present system works. This demonstrates understanding of present operating systems and establishes credibility.

4. **Alternatives:** Describe alternate viable solutions.
   A...
   B...
   C...

5. **Analyses and Evaluations:**
   Technical and strategic summaries of non-quantifiable issues.
   Financial and economic summaries and comparisons.

6. **Conclusion and Recommendation:**
   Summarize and recommend the appropriate solution and why.
   Discuss project sensitivity and equipment utilization levels.

7. **Appendices:** (Supporting documentation that must be readily available)
   Detailed cost analyses and summaries of:
   Capital and program costs
   Operating costs and expenses
   Discounted cash flow analysis schedules
   Implementation plan and schedule
   Reference articles from publications
   Vendor and supplier product catalogs
   System bids and quotations
   System specifications

8. **Visual Aids:** Charts, graphs, slides, films, hand-outs, spreadsheets.

Explanation of Project Format Outline

Part 1 Program Title, Dollar Amount, and Reference Number:

Program Title or Name:
Name the project. Keep it short, general, and generic, and do not use manufacturers names or model numbers.

Avoid using specifics such as capacity, size, horsepower, etc. as much as possible. These variables may change as the project finalizes, and the differences, although justified, can be time consuming and difficult to explain.

Examples:

Correct	Incorrect
Metal Removal Cell	Two Six Pallet (Brand Name) Horizontal Machining Centers
Robot Welding Cell	Six Axis Robot, 400 Amp MIG Welding System, With Two Indexing Positioners

More specific and lengthy titles will attract more attention than necessary, and will probably not enhance the chances of success for the project in any way.

Total Dollar Amount:
The total amount of dollars required to implement the project, rounded to the nearest $100. Show the number without cents, and remember that too many zeros scare people.

Examples:	Correct	Incorrect
	$156,400	$156,400.00
		$156,397.40

Approval of the funds does not require that they be expressed in precise amounts at this time.

Reference Number: This number is used for budgeting, accounting, tracking, and project control.

Project Outline

Part 2 Synopsis/Summary:

Write a brief paragraph describing the project concept, definitely less than one page.

See the examples in Chapter Nine.

Part 3 Problem/Opportunity Statement:

Background:
Describe the relevant issues associated with current means of satisfying the needs. Among them will be lack of adequate capacity, poor quality, obsolescence, high operating and maintenance cost, poor response time, competitive disadvantage, advancements in technology, and others.

Present System Description:
Detail the present system, outlining the specific areas for possible improvement. This definition of the existing circumstances demonstrates the level of understanding of current manufacturing systems, and establishes credibility and confidence in the project proposal.

Part 4 Alternatives:

Define each of the most realistic and viable alternatives in enough detail to establish their functionality. Don't forget to include doing nothing, or modifications or rebuild of the present system as one of the alternatives. Do not offer more than three or four alternatives at the most because this will over-complicate the proposal and the decision process, and it will be extremely difficult to clearly identify and substantiate the viability of all the possible alternatives.

The decision makers realize that there are always minor differences within alternatives, and all of the possibilities and variations need not be discussed in the proposal. There just isn't enough room or time to wade through all of that information.

Part 5 Analyses and Evaluations

This section includes comparative analyses of both strategic and quantitative issues related to the present system, as well as the alternatives.

The form of this information is important. It should be in summary form, presented as spreadsheets, or graphic illustrations suitable for handouts or projection slides.

Each document must be self-explanatory. Even though they may be accompanied with verbal explanations at the time of presentation, opportunity for the clarification will not always be available.

The relative advantages and disadvantages of the present system, and various alternatives should be clearly evident.

Don't miss any relevant issues. Your credibility is at stake.

Part 6 Conclusion and Recommendation:

While the decision makers will make the final decision, they are definitely interested in your knowledgeable opinion, and an intelligent consensus view of what should be done.

The conclusion and recommendation should be clear and obvious, justified with supporting arguments, and not too wordy.

Say what must be said, and get on with the program.

Part 7 Appendices:

The amount of supporting information provided with the proposal depends on who wants to see what, when, and where. In any case, the information must be made available when needed, to all who require it, in comprehensive and understandable form.

In conclusion, It should go without saying, but won't, that all information obtained and developed for the project proposal should be considered proprietary, be held in confidence, and should not be made available to second or third parties without acquiring appropriate consent to release the information.

Getting the Preliminary Approvals

The proposals being offered to the board for their consideration have most likely been under discussion for some time. When a proposal is brought before the board their positions on the project are probably already known by most participants. There should be no surprises.

Nobody likes surprises, especially decision makers.

One way to avoid surprises, especially at the final stage, is to provide preliminary information about the project to the other decision makers' groups. Invite their critical analyses of the data ahead of time so that all concerns and issues can be brought to the surface, and dealt with in a timely and effective manner.

The three primary areas where preliminary approvals are especially valuable (probably even essential) are **finance**, **production**, and the **executives**. Certainly other areas and departments also have significant interests in what is being proposed, but any of the above-mentioned groups probably have a flat veto power over the project. If they don't agree with, or oppose the project, they may even have an alternative up their sleeve. It is best to find out early in the process if this is the case, so that these issues can be resolved. Find out whose support for the program will be forthcoming, and who will need more persuasion.

It is especially helpful, (practically essential), that the concerns of all who may be involved or affected by the project be requested, and obtained as early as possible in the project. This way all of the issues, questions and concerns of all groups can be addressed, and hopefully resolved before the final proposal is submitted.

The Presentation . . . Are You Ready?

Don't do it if you're not. Your credibility is at stake.

The following is a checklist of things to have done before taking the project to the board of directors or executive committee to request their approval. They deserve nothing less.

Be organized.

Make no mistakes.

Make sure **all** the arithmetic works.

The presentation is professionally done.

Keep the proposal as generic as possible.

Be sure that all documentation and statements are completely accurate and truthful.

Have visual aids and handouts available (Slides, Charts, etc.)

Be available, and be able to answer all questions.

Know what you're talking about or have immediate access to an expert.

Know what your competition is doing in this area.
    (You will probably be asked.)

Have quotes available from key affected parties if possible.
    (e.g. "Production says they like the proposal.")

Keep to the point, be brief, and don't waste their time.

Sell the program, and ask for their approval.

Be available at any time for the presentation

7

It's Decision Time . . .
JUST DO IT.

Keeping a project journal where relevant project activity is recorded chronologically is a very valuable reference tool.

Just Do It.

Now that all the research, analysis, and preparations are done, it's time to proceed with the decision process.

It is important to understand the implications of the project thoroughly, and the positions (points of view) held by the various parties who will be involved in the decision.

> **Knowing in advance, the issues that will be in question by the decision makers, allows proper preparation of responses and answers for those questions.**

Being able to answer effectively, all of the questions and issues raised during the review meetings can mean the difference between approval and deferring or delaying the project.

If we've done our job, there should be no questions left unanswered, and a favorable decision to proceed with the project will be forthcoming.

Getting things done . . . **being a "doer"** . . . is a reputation to be highly valued. Especially when projects are approved, implemented, meet performance expectations, and come in under budget. This is what establishes credibility.

> **Guard your credibility and integrity jealously.**

Carrying successful experiences as an effective project manager into a project review meeting is a significant asset. People will "listen when you talk" and seriously consider your perspectives and proposals.

But . . . preparation is absolutely required.

> **You must be ready going in.**

You have only just begun the task.

Now it's time, and you must proceed to the next step . . .

The Executive Committee

Now is the time for decision.

With the presentation and all the supporting documentation ready, it's time for the decision makers to do their job.

This process can take many forms. For purposes of this discussion however, the project proposal and recommendation will be presented to an "executive committee." We may even be fortunate enough to have all the interested parties present.

Remember that these are very busy people. Their time is in great demand, and the fact that one or more of the decision makers may not be present should not be discouraging. It's best to assume that they would have been there if possible. If one or more of the members can't make it, they will probably send someone in their place, or make their position known ahead of time to one or more of the other parties at the meeting.

The time of the meeting may also be indefinite. It may be scheduled at 2:00 pm, but this may not be the only issue on the meeting agenda. It is possible that discussion of this project may be delayed because of other items on the agenda. You will probably not be present for the entire meeting, only that portion directly related to your project proposal. But be ready at any time. You may be called into the meeting early, or late, or might even be rescheduled because of some other subject which has taken an unexpected amount of time.

Don't panic. This is normal.

Keep things in perspective. This project is obviously a number one priority to you, but it is probably just one of many very important issues on the executive committee agenda for their consideration.

Be patient. Your time will come.

And when it does, be ready, be positive, and . . . **Go for it.**

So you finally make it into the meeting. Now is the time.

It's important to know who the key participants are, and their positions on the issues in advance. This is just part of being prepared for the meeting. There should be no surprises.

Be sure the project is understood by all parties, but remember their time is very valuable, so don't drag out the issues or bore the folks with endless statistics and concepts that they can study at their own convenience, or may already know.

Avoid using cliches, especially ones that turn people off.

Saying things like "it's state of the art," or "Everybody else does it this way," or other similar expressions that generalize and oversimplify concepts don't build credibility, and frequently deny the realities of the issues. It's known as the "broad-brush" approach, and it doesn't work.

Remember why you are there, stay focused, be specific, and do what you came there to do. Explain the program, answer their questions, then let the executive committee do their job. (Make the decision.)

Some principles and benefits to explain and emphasize during the meeting if you have time, and only if they specifically apply are:

- How you're doing it now
- How you propose to do it better
- Why and how quality will be easier to manage
- How much it will cost
- Show the implementation plan
- How it satisfies the capital program investment criteria for:
  - Return on investment
  - Payback period
  - Net present value
- How the program reduces direct operating expenses

The Executive Committee

    Where the annual savings come from

    Reduces material costs

    Reduces labor cost

    Reduces cost of supplies

    Reduces sub-contract costs

    How it improves long term cash flow

    How the program reduces inventory levels

    Reduces inventory carrying costs

    Reduces material handling costs

    Reduces maintenance expenses

    Improves response time

    Reduces freight costs

    Offers greater flexibility

    Reduces space requirements

    Show how the customer will benefit

    Show how the employees will benefit

    Show how the stockholder will benefit

    Show how your corporate image will be improved

    Any other disadvantages or advantages? State those too

    What other strategic advantages? Be specific

Pick and choose the most Important.

See appendix B for more food for thought.

Getting Final Approval

Getting the final approval for a project is a very gratifying experience.

Having the appropriate documentation ready in advance for the principal signatures of approval is very important. When they are ready to put their signatures on the dotted line, it's best to have all the appropriate documentation ready.

Don't be afraid to ask for the approval. It's hard to imagine a salesman who ever got an order who didn't ask for it first.

Even though you may have brought the paperwork into the meeting, leave the primary paperwork with your boss, and let them get any remaining signatures, if needed.

When you receive the completed documentation, this will be the official authorization to go ahead with the project.

> **But, don't spend the money yet . . .**

As with most projects, the work is only just beginning. The approval of the project in principle may, or may not be authorization to spend the money. If large expenditures of funds are planned, specific requisitions and purchase orders or contracts may require individual approval, usually by the department, or division head.

Getting the project approval is a real milestone and accomplishment. Congratulations are in order for both yourself and your associates. There should be no turning back now.

Be sure to advise your associates that the project has been approved as soon as you can. They will be as thrilled as you are to learn of the approval, and will look forward to the implementation of the new program.

But, there is still a lot of specific work to be done before you can begin to spend the money, as will be seen in the next section.

On with implementation. Now you can make it happen.

OK . . . But Don't Spend the Money Yet

Now that funds have officially been approved for the project, the clock can start on the long lead-time activities such as equipment acquisitions, facilities modifications, training, and support Systems Development.

But first, you must finalize the system design, equipment specifications, and acquisition terms with the potential suppliers. Let them know they must still be competitive with their offering, and the equipment order is definitely **not** "in the bag".

This will probably be your last chance to review the final system specifications before it is purchased, with the people who will have to make it work. Don't miss this opportunity. Have them look it over with you, and make any final comments and recommendations. Resolve **all** the open issues, and make any final adjustments to the system specifications that may be necessary. If changes are required to the system later, they can and will be very expensive. Believe it.

> **Now is the time during the project when you have the greatest leverage with your suppliers.**

Now is the time to get the best possible value from the suppliers. This does not mean to beat them over their heads. The terms agreed upon at this time will become the final purchase order or contract, and must be good for both you and your suppliers. Be aware, that there are many ways to improve your position with your suppliers and vendors. Failure to take advantage of these circumstances at this time is a real mistake.

Purchasing agents, while not necessarily involved directly in the technical specifications of major equipment purchases, will be of tremendous value at this time in terms of helping to finalize those specifications, and conditions of the purchase order or contract, such as payment terms, discounts, and delivery schedules.

Investigating the financial stability and integrity of the potential suppliers is another important responsibility that can be absorbed by the purchasing agents. They can request Dunn and Bradstreet (D&B) reports, which will give an indication of the financial stability of the potential suppliers of the equipment. If you haven't worked with a particular supplier before, this summary can be very revealing.

Implementation

Although the next chapter is all about making it happen, the implementation of the project requires considerable cooperation from many quarters, as you will see.

To begin with, implementing the project by definition involves change.

> **Change is difficult and hard for people, especially if their job is directly impacted by the project.**

Just some of the questions they will ask are:

> Is my job going to change?
> Will I have to learn new skills?
> Will I be able to learn them?
> Will I be transferred to another department?
> Will I even have a job when this is all over?

These are serious questions, especially for a person who has been on the job, year after year, is very specialized, has an excellent work record, and may be displaced by new, more advanced technology.

> **Change can be a threat to anyone.**

> **Specific answers to the above questions, as well as others must be available.**

A project implementation schedule or plan is an essential part of the program. It shows the things that have to get done, and when they are expected to happen. It is an event driven document.

A good implementation plan or schedule helps demonstrate the thoroughness, that was applied in analyzing the project, and adds to the overall credibility of the program analysis.

But remember, it is only a plan, and subject to change based on actual timing of events. It can be used as an overall guide, and is a good tool to use to keep people informed on the progress of the project.

The next page shows a basic example of an implementation schedule.

Project Implementation Schedule

ID	Activity	Apr	May	Jun	Jul	Aug	Sep	Oct	Nov
1	**Project Approval**	XX							
2	**Finalize Specifications**	XX							
3	**Equipment Acquisition**		X						
4	Purchase		X						
5	Construction		XXXXXXXX						
6	Delivery				X				
7	Installation					XX			
8	Start Up					X			
9	Run Off						XI		
10	**Fixtures**						I		
11	Specifications	XXX					I		
12	Acquisition		XXXXXXXXXXXXXXX				I		
13	Set Up					XXX	I		
14	**Tooling**						I		
15	Specifications	XXX					I		
16	Acquisition		XXXXXXXXXX				I		
17	Set Up				XXX		I		
18	**Personnel Training**						I		
19	Maintenance			XX	XX		I		
20	Operator				XX	XX	I		
21	**Computer Support**						I		
22	Hardware Specs/Dev		XXXXXX				I		
23	Software Specs/Dev		XXXXXX				I		
24	HW/SW Integration			XXXXXX			I		
25	Fixtures/Tooling Integ.				XXX		I		
26	HW/SW/MT Debug					XXX	I		
27	**System Start Up**						IX		
28	**System Run-off**							X	
29	**System Run-off**							XX	
30	**Production**								XXX
31	**Audit**	starts six weeks post production startup							

Project Implementation Schedule (Basic Example)

Critical Task: **XXXX**

Task: XXXX

Date:

By:

> **It will work . . . Believe in it.**

The new technology will work, work well, and be more productive.

It will cost less in the long run and do all the things it is supposed to do.

> **And . . . it will displace people.**

It's the nature of maintaining the competitive advantage in the marketplace, the manufacturing environment, and staying in business.

It is the root to . . . *UNLEASHING PRODUCTIVITY*.

The prescriptions for manufacturing survival, (improvements in manufacturing technology) **will** increase productivity, and **will** help increase company growth through increased market share and lower manufacturing costs.

The manufacturing organization can easily absorb the jobs that are displaced by higher productivity if the potential increased market share is realized.

> **It is the companies that *fail* to improve productivity that will lose the jobs. . .**
>
> **. . . not the companies that become more competitive through better manufacturing technology and systems, and absorb displaced jobs through better utilization and higher thruput.**

Now . . . on with making it happen.

8

Making It Happen . . .

Engineering the cost of materials, and/or labor operations out of the product, without compromising product functionality, or customer acceptance, are the surest and easiest ways of reducing product cost.

Making It Happen

Now that you've done the preliminaries, and your homework, by laying the groundwork for introducing the new systems, making it happen should progress smoothly, and in a very positive way.

It is important to **have a plan** for the implementation of the new system, showing the timing related to the training of personnel, the start of re-arrangement of facilities, arrival and installation of the new equipment, start-up, run-off, and other significant steps involved in implementing the new technology.

The implementation plan can be updated regularly, and copies given to the people directly affected by the changes. Keep everyone informed as to the progress of the project, and be prepared to answer lots of questions with factual and accurate information.

> **Communications with all parties directly affected by the project is essential for successful installation and start-up of the new technology . . . share the plan.**

Implementing the Technology

To begin with, make sure all those directly involved with the project **understand** what's going to happen, when it's going to happen, and how it's going to work.

> **This is essential to the success of the program.**

It will probably involve some meetings, or question and answer sessions about the new systems, with all those both directly and indirectly involved.

Make sure they understand the new system. This is their hour of need, and more importantly . . .

> **Don't abandon them.**

Change Is Tough

Remember . . .

> **If they don't understand it . . . it probably won't work as well as it should, or may not even work at all.**

Take the time required to explain and answer **all** questions, and make sure all parties understand the new system, what is expected of them, and how to make it work.

Changing is Tough

The challenge of change is tough for everybody. If the people implementing the new systems are insensitive to those directly affected by the changes, it can make it really hard on all concerned.

And don't forget the people whose jobs are going away, they too must adjust to new requirements and job demands.

> **Change is tough for anybody.**

Being transferred to another department, getting to know new people, having a new supervisor, or even working a different shift, are just a few of the adjustment demands we place on the people.

At the risk of being redundant . . . *changing is tough!*

Final Specifications and Quotations

Even though the suppliers have submitted proposals quoting their system specifications, price and delivery conditions, these must be reviewed again to make sure nothing has been missed.

> **Get together again with all the people who will be operating and maintaining the new system for another review.**

Make sure all the bases are covered.

The field of potential suppliers has by now probably been narrowed to not more than two or three. Now you get down to the short strokes.

The selection of the system supplier will be made based on these final negotiations. Invite the potential vendors in for final discussions, and:

Definitely . . . Absolutely . . . A must do . . .

> **Involve your purchasing group in these meetings.**

As the purchaser, you will **never** have more leverage than at this time.

> **You must take advantage of this opportunity.**
>
> **You are not doing your job if you don't.**

Depending on the supplier, several incentives may be reasonably extracted from the vendor in exchange for the order that day. Some of the possibilities are listed here:

> Additional useful equipment options
> Extended warranty periods
> Additional start-up help
> Additional personnel training
> More favorable payment terms
> One last additional price concession

I'm sure you get the idea, and the vendors probably have a few ideas of their own to contribute, especially if they want the order.

Keep in mind that the suppliers are probably expecting this pressure for additional concessions. They have been there before . . . but so have you. This is not the first time for either of you, and it will not be the last, and the vendor knows you're serious.

Be ready to negotiate, and put the deal together.

> **Hint: Have more of your people at the meeting than they do.**

Good luck.

Vendor Selection

Now that the specifications are all finalized, and you have received the final commitments and proposals from the suppliers. Pick the winner.

Have several very good reasons why you selected the particular vendor you did, and some very good reasons for not selecting the ones you didn't. (You will be asked.)

Advise the winner they got the order and why. They will obviously be happy to hear the good news. (This is the fun part.)

Now, the hard part. (This is part of why you get paid.)

You are obliged as a matter of business courtesy to advise those who did not get the order, that they were not selected as the system supplier.

You **do not** have to tell them who did get the order. (They will find out eventually anyway.) and, you should **definitely not** divulge any of the specific terms or conditions that you've negotiated with your supplier of choice. **This is proprietary information.**

You can and should tell them of any specific technical reasons why their equipment offer or proposal was not selected. This will have the overall long-term effect of helping them, and others, to better configure systems proposals for their customers in the future.

You can indicate whether price was a primary determining factor and whether they were high, low, or competitive, but do not indicate how much. (They will definitely feel better if they find out their bid was higher than their competitor who did get the order.)

Remember that the vendors who didn't get the order will probably have to go back home to their managers and explain why they didn't get it. That's the cruel reality of the matter. If you're the sales person, that's really the tough part.

Depending on the supplier, you can expect to receive various responses from them about the fact that they did not receive the order.

Some of the vendors will accept your decision and go on about their business.

My experience has been that the stronger companies, the ones who know their costs, their business, and their market best will be in this category.

But, some will complain a lot, and even go to your management to inform them of your in-appropriate decision. They may ask to re-quote the project, especially if their price was padded in the first place.

> **Do not allow them the opportunity to re-quote the job.**

I guarantee some suppliers will want that opportunity, but they should have taken their best shot going in, and if they didn't, they should have learned from that, too.

They may come back with "well we made a mistake, and . . . etc."

Don't buy it. They had their shot.

Equipment Acquisition

Once the equipment is on order, it is important to keep in touch with the equipment supplier to provide any information or assistance he may need in a timely way. Stay on top of this.

> **Now is not the time for surprises to start.** (Never is better.)

Make sure the supplier stays on schedule, and has all the answers he needs immediately.

> **Look over his shoulder, and keep your eyes and ears open.**

At the appropriate time, you may need to make arrangements (contact an equipment carrier) for delivery of the equipment to your site. If special transportation permits, licensing, or transportation equipment is needed, these may require a few days to a few weeks to put in place.

Computer Support

The information required to support manufacturing systems can best be managed by a computer. It's definitely faster and more accurate than the manual alternative. This is no revelation. It's just a fact of life these days.

The extent of the computer support required, however, will be determined by the degree, level of automation, and specialized information and control variables required by the production system.

In some cases, the information support system will operate completely in the background, and you will hardly know it's there. However, in other applications, it may be highly interactive, and very visible.

Most likely the computer and information support system will be somewhere in between for your application. These variables, both hardware and software, must be thoroughly defined, and be included as part of the overall operating system costs and specifications. Remember this. . .

> **Computers do what they do best.**
> **People do what they do best.**
> **Machines do what they do best.**
>
> **and, <u>don't let them get in each other's way!</u>**

Too frequently, the shoe is put on the wrong foot so to speak, and that's not very much fun, or comfortable for anybody. And, besides being uncomfortable, it doesn't work.

Computer support systems do a good job, are very flexible, and not particularly expensive these days, but remember . . .

> **Whatever you put in place, you will have to maintain.**

Remember you heard this somewhere, when you want or need to change some of the operating parameters embedded in your support software, or you can't get replacement boards for your obsolete machine controller any more. You will have to step up to the newer technology.

Operations and Maintenance Training

Installing new manufacturing technology without providing adequate training for the equipment operators and maintenance personnel more than compromises the potential productivity of the system. It invites chaos, and is a potential disaster waiting to happen.

> **Somebody has to know how to run the system.**

And. . .

> **Somebody has to know how to fix it when it breaks.**

System operators and maintenance personnel training are an essential part of any new installation. They may be paid for and written off as part of a training budget, and therefore not included as part of the capital cost of the system, but the training is absolutely essential and must be planned and included as part of the overall program cost.

> **Timing is important.**

Training of system operators and maintenance personnel should be done just prior to the installation of the equipment, and not too long before it's actually ready to run on the floor. This timing will maximize the effectiveness of the learning experience.

> **If training takes place too soon, the personnel will probably forget most of what they learned before they even get a chance to apply it.**

The equipment suppliers and computer support personnel not only must provide the system documentation and operation manuals, but are excellent sources for the training required to assure complete understanding of how the system works, and how to fix it when necessary.

A good training program for operators and maintenance personnel will help assure a smooth start-up of the system, and provide the confidence to the operators and maintenance personnel, that they know what they are doing, and that they will be able to fix it and keep it running if something goes wrong.

System Installation

If you're concerned about the new system attracting attention, this phase of the project will surely put those concerns to rest. People will come out of the woodwork to see what is going on, and there will be several Monday morning quarterbacks to offer advice about what should be done instead of what you are doing. Be prepared to answer lots of questions, and give lots of explanations about why the system is configured the way it is. Most importantly . . . **Be there**.

Make sure you are ready. If you're not, it's too late. It's going to happen anyway, and you will simply have to struggle through it.

All the site preparation work including the foundations, support utilities, etc., must be ready for the equipment installation.

Computer support hardware and software must be ready for installation.

When the equipment arrives, make sure it is handled and installed with strict adherence to the equipment suppliers specifications. You must comply with all handling and installation criteria supplied by the equipment builder. It can, and will affect your equipment warranties if not done properly.

If possible, have your maintenance personnel involved in the equipment installation and start-up procedures. This will give them valuable initial exposure and experience with the equipment.

Get the equipment supplier to inspect, and buy-off on the installation.

They should be the first ones to power up the equipment.

There should be no surprises, but you never know.

Even though the equipment is at your site, it's the suppliers job to get the equipment running the way it should before your operators get involved with the machines.

Have the supplier confirm that the equipment installation has been completed to their satisfaction, and the system is ready to perform.

Start-Up and Testing

After the equipment is installed, accuracies and other performance criteria confirmed, and other equipment tests performed, the supplier will say the system is ready to run your parts.

Sometimes, machine testing is scheduled to take place at the suppliers factory prior to shipment. This procedure may be used to demonstrate the capability of the equipment for the customer prior to shipment.

Your parts, with your fixtures, your tooling, and your programming, can now be processed on the equipment. Proper operation of the system must be demonstrated to your satisfaction, and if you have questions, or are dissatisfied with any part of the system, now is the time to resolve those issues. Document and advise all appropriate parties your concerns and follow up with solutions.

Get your operators fully involved in this startup phase.

Remember, there is a learning curve here, and it can take several weeks for the system operators to get familiar with the new equipment. They must learn how the equipment responds to input variable changes, so that they can develop a reasonable confidence level in their own abilities, and fully understand the capabilities of the equipment.

Have the system supplier show you how to make the system work best for you. Ask them specifically, where, how, and what changes they would recommend in your programming, fixtures, or tooling to maximize the performance of the system. **Get their input.** They have a lot of experience and industry exposure that can probably be applied to your parts. They will be happy to share their ideas with you if you ask them.

Be patient. Start up one job at a time.

When tuning the job programs, don't change too many variables at one time. (Sometimes one is too many.) This can easily result in more confusion than you need to confront for the time being.

Get the jobs running so that **manual intervention is minimized or eliminated** throughout the production cycle, then go on to the next job.

Production Run Off

After several of the jobs have been tuned to run as they should, move into a production mode where different jobs are run back-to-back, so that machine utilization can be maximized.

Run in this production mode continuously for an extended period of time and shake the system down, (several hours at least). Watch for system constraints that cause delays, manual intervention, or shut downs, and track the causes. Find as many glitches in the system as possible over a period of time, then shut the system down and fix them.

Then start another shakedown run.

Keep going through this procedure until the system is responding with continuous production demands without delays or shutdowns.

> **The system should run without faults. After all, it's brand new.**

Make it run the way it's supposed to . . . and keep it running that way.

The Audit

Have the new system operate in a production mode for several weeks. Make sure all the bugs are fixed.

> ***Then*, invite your internal audit group to check it out.**

They will verify that the system performance meets projections and expectations and will report back to management that you spent their money well, and did a good job.

This audit will demonstrate and confirm your credibility as a system designer, installer, and integrator.

> **Almost everyone will be impressed.**

There are always a few people who won't be impressed by anything.

Typical Project Cash Flow Summary

The cash flows generated by the decision to proceed with the project will follow a fairly predictable pattern.

The chart on the next page reflects the approximate timing of cash flows for a typical project. The cash flows are shown as cumulative by quarter, and reflects anticipated expenses and savings, and the resulting net cash flows for three years, by quarter.

It reflects an investment of $750,000, which generates a $100,000 per quarter after tax savings. The savings, realistically, do not start until after the equipment is installed during the third quarter, and is fully operational. The chart also reflects a learning curve or period of about three to six months to allow the operators to come up to speed on the system. The break-even point, or payback period, is approximately two and a half years, and it takes about one year to fully implement the system.

The outgoing cash flows for the program will begin shortly after the project is released for implementation because equipment suppliers will usually require some up-front funds to begin work on the system. Most of the capital funds for the project will be expended by the time the equipment is shipped and installed, but some funds should be held back until after the system is fully operational, and achieves the projected objectives and capabilities.

Notice that the chart reasonably reflects the startup period, or learning curve. This doesn't start until after the equipment is completely installed. Then it usually takes about six months to get a new manufacturing system up to speed, (depending on complexity) before the estimated benefits will be fully realized.

Cash Flow

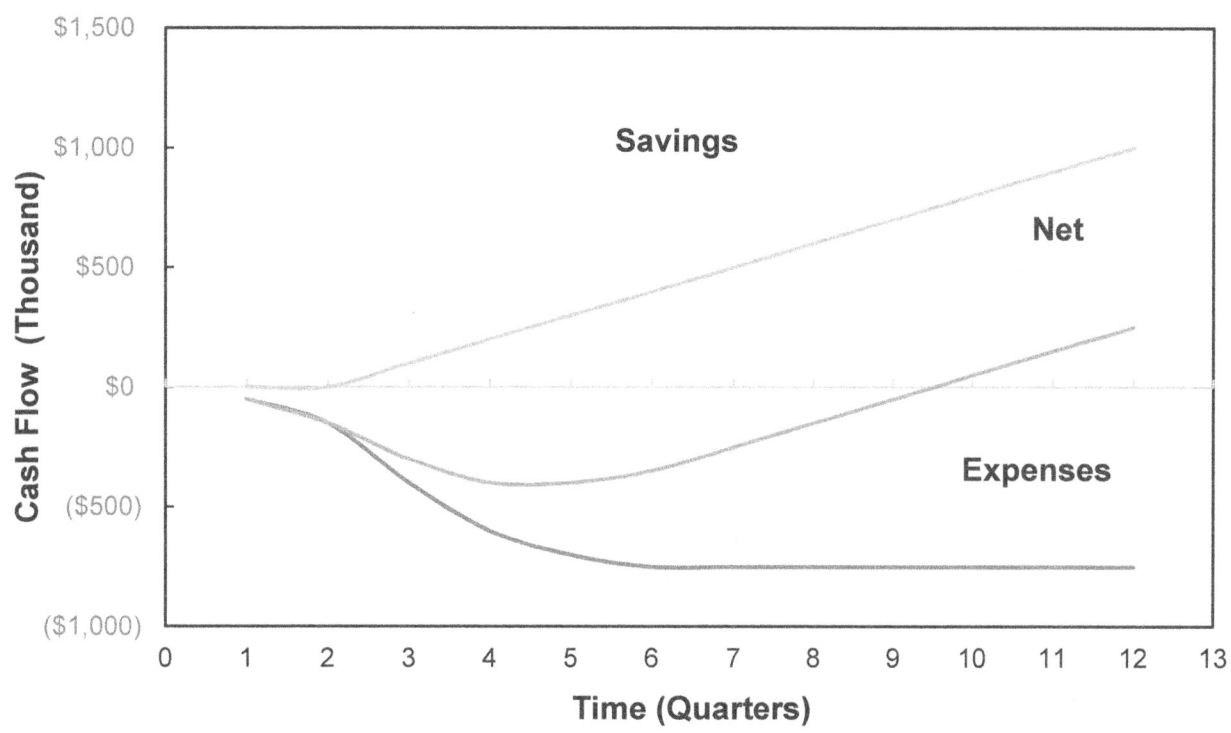

Time (Quarters)	Cumulative Cash Flow		
	Expenses	Savings	Net
1	(50,000)	-	(50,000)
2	(150,000)	-	(150,000)
3	(400,000)	100,000	(300,000)
4	(600,000)	200,000	(400,000)
5	(700,000)	300,000	(400,000)
6	(750,000)	400,000	(350,000)
7	(750,000)	500,000	(250,000)
8	(750,000)	600,000	(150,000)
9	(750,000)	700,000	(50,000)
10	(750,000)	800,000	50,000
11	(750,000)	900,000	150,000
12	(750,000)	1,000,000	250,000

9

Examples and Applications

The potential residual value of assets are frequently overlooked, or not even considered, in the financial justification phase of a project or program.

Double Your Pleasure . . . Double Your Fun

Productivity improvements do not happen by accident.

It takes planning, commitment, effort, support from management, and cooperation from all involved parties, including vendors.

You can double your productivity too.

This chapter offers three specific summary scenarios for improving manufacturing productivity in the areas of Metal Removal, Metal Fabrication, and Robot Welding Systems, as well as the computer support requirements to help maximize the benefits of the systems.

The detailed documentation supporting the savings and expenditure requirements are omitted because they are so dependent on the specific application, but the overall benefits and costs outlined in the programs are valid representations of what can be expected.

The program proposals on the following pages are real. They represent actual manufacturing systems that were approved by executive committees or boards of directors, have been installed, are in full production, and have been fully audited for performance. These systems are now fully operational in several companies that have demonstrated their commitment to . . .

unleashing their productivity.

Your company can do it too.

A brief note on computer support systems . . .

Generally speaking, major improvements in productivity can be achieved without computer support systems if the product mix and variability are relatively low. But, if the product mix and variability are high, then the benefits of a good computer support system become readily apparent, and very necessary.

Metal Removal System
(Proposal)

July 4, 1995
Tim Fleskes

Program Title: **Metal Removal System**

Reference Number: (Fill this in as needed)

Program Amount: **$1,250,000**

Synopsis:

Recent developments in metal removal systems and technology offer the opportunity to greatly improve and upgrade our own in-house metal removal equipment and manufacturing systems. This newer technology is proven and currently used in several manufacturing facilities throughout the country.

This proposal outlines a new metal removal system scenario for our applications which will result in higher productivity, lower inventories, faster response time, better quality, and reduced product cost.

The strategic and economic advantages are significant. Based on two shift utilization of the proposed system, the projected annual savings of **$249,000** per year and other cash flow benefits generate an **after-tax** return on investment of **16.3%** with a net present value of **$655,604** and payback period of **3.1 years**.

Background:

Our present metal removal systems include machine tools which require continuous monitoring by operators in order to assure essential product quality and thruput. In addition, our fixtures and tooling are highly part specific and not expected to support the long term demands for increased flexibility and higher production volumes.

Since each machine tool presently requires an operator, the utilization of the machine and the operator are both compromised by the fact that generally, the machine can't get any work done while the operators are doing their job, and neither can the operators get much done while the machine is doing its work. The current operator to machine ratio is typically one to one.

Set-up times alone for the jobs under the current system absorb from 10% to 25% of the time required to manufacture the parts. Many parts require several separate set-ups and operations to complete the required work. This present manufacturing system forces greater lead times through the shop, and higher material, work in process, and finished goods inventories.

Metal Removal System Proposal

Our present machine tools are aged and worn, and require frequent maintenance attention in an effort to keep them running the way they should. They frequently break down at the most inopportune times (just when we need them the most), and service and replacement parts are not readily available if at all.

Alternatives:

Three basic alternatives are presented for your consideration:

A: Present System (Do nothing)

Doing nothing is the easiest, but nothing will improve. Manufacturing costs will continue to increase, not decrease. Product quality will become even more difficult to maintain, and thruput will be limited to what can be produced with the current equipment and technology on hand.

B: Farm Out

Metal removal operations can be farmed out or out-sourced to sub-contractors, but at a significant cost premium, as will be seen in the following summaries. This alternative carries with it several strategic and economic disadvantages including lack of control, and questionable long-term cost stability.

C: New Metal Removal System

This alternative replaces existing equipment with newer technology. Among the principal benefits are reduced labor, inventories, and material handling. The new machine tools do not require continuous operator attendance, and flexibility and response time are improved significantly.

The new machines can operate unattended through coffee breaks, lunch periods, and shift changes. Both the operator and machine tools operate independently of each other because of appropriate job queuing using multiple machine pallet strategy. The operator to machine ratio is reduced to one to two or better.

Raw material, work in process, and finished goods inventories are minimized because **set-up time is eliminated**, and all of the work required on the parts is done, basically in one continuous machine sequence including manual deburring operations. Rough parts go in and finished parts come out with every pallet cycle. Lead time is greatly reduced and there are no partially completed parts (work in process) on the shop floor.

Comparison Of Alternatives
(Based On Two Shift Operation)

Alternative Item Description	A Present System	B Farm Out	C New System
Number of machines	4	N/A	2
Number of people required	8	N/A	2
Hours per year per machine	4,000	N/A	4,000
Total hours available per year	16,000	N/A	8,000
Average equipment utilization	45%	N/A	90%
Net metal cutting hours per year	7,200	7,200	7,200
Set up hours per year	4,000	N/A	0
Operator cost per hour	$20.00	N/A	$20.00
Hours per year per operator	2,000	N/A	2,000
Labor cost per year	$320,000	$540,000	$80,000
Cost per metal cutting hour	$44.44	$75.00	$11.11
Annual savings:	None	($220,000)	**$240,000**
Material Handling			
Annual cost	$15,000	$0	$10,000
Annual savings:	None	$15,000	**$5,000**
Inventories			
Inventory turns per year	10	20	50
Average inventory value	$50,000	$25,000	$10,000
One time inventory reduction	None	$25,000	**$40,000**
Carrying costs @ 10%	$5,000	$2,500	$1,000
Annual savings:	None	$2,500	**$4,000**
Total annual savings:	None	($202,500)	**$249,000**

Conclusion And Recommendation

Proceed with the implementation of alternative C, the new metal removal system, and recover the benefits as outlined.

Metal Removal System
Discounted Cash Flow Summary

Item Description	Time Now	Year 1	Year 2	Year 3	Year 4	Year 5
Program Costs						
Equipment	$950,000					
Fixtures	175,000					
Expenses	125,000					
Total:	$1,250,000					
Cash Flows						
Depreciation		$247,750	$381,000	$220,750	$142,500	$133,000
Reduced Inventories		25,000	15,000			
Residual Value of Equipment						300,000
Annual Savings		200,000	249,000	249,000	249,000	249,000
Taxes	38%	76,000	94,620	94,620	94,620	94,620
Tax Credit*	10%	N/A				
After Tax Earnings						
Future Values		$396,750	$550,380	$375,130	$296,880	$587,380
Discount Rate Per Year		5.0%				
Present Values		$377,858	$499,213	$324,054	$244,247	$460,232
Program Summary (After Tax)						
Net Present Value		$655,604				
Internal Rate Of Return		16.3%				
Payback Period (Years)		3.2				

Table reflects 1995 data, however 2025 would be 70% to 75% higher due to inflation.

Cost of materials, labor, and equipment will have increased accordingly; however, this would have little impact on the program justification itself.

Metal Fabrication System
(Proposal)

July 4, 1995
Tim Fleskes

Program Title: **Metal Fabrication System**

Reference Number: (Fill this in as needed)

Program Amount: **$1,500,000**

Synopsis:

Recent developments in metal fabrication systems and technology offer the opportunity to greatly improve and upgrade our own in-house metal fabrication equipment and manufacturing systems. This newer technology is **proven** and currently used in several manufacturing facilities throughout the country.

The proposal outlines a new metal fabrication system scenario for our applications, which will result in higher productivity, lower inventories, faster response time, better quality, and reduced product cost.

The strategic and economic advantages are significant. Based on two shift utilization of the proposed system, the projected annual savings of **$487,000** per year and other cash flow benefits generate an **after-tax** return on investment of **21.1%** with a net present value of **$1,070,664** and payback period of **2.8** years.

Background:

Our present metal fabrication systems include equipment which is antiquated, and requires continuous monitoring by operators in order to assure essential product quality and thruput. And in addition, will not provide the anticipated increased demands for greater flexibility and higher production volumes.

Since each production machine now requires an operator, the utilization of the machine and the operator are both compromised by the fact that generally, the machines can't get any work done while the operators are doing their job, and neither can the operators get much done while the machine is doing its work. The current operator to machine ratio is typically one to one.

Set-up times alone for the jobs under the current system absorb from 10% to 25% of the time required to manufacture the parts. Many parts require several separate set-ups and operations to complete the required work. This present type of manufacturing system forces greater lead times through the shop, and more raw material, work in process and finished goods inventories.

Metal Fabrication System Proposal

Our present equipment is aged and worn, and requires frequent maintenance attention in an effort to keep it running the way it should. The equipment frequently breaks down at the most in-opportune times (just when we need them the most), and service and replacement parts are not readily available if at all.

Alternatives:

Three basic alternatives are presented for your consideration:

A: Present System (Do nothing)

Doing nothing is the easiest, but nothing will improve. Manufacturing costs will continue to increase, not decrease. Product quality will become even more difficult to maintain, and thruput will be limited to what can be produced with the current equipment and technology on hand.

B: Farm Out

Metal fabrication operations can be farmed out or out-sourced to sub-contractors, but at a significant cost premium, as will be seen in the following summaries. This alternative carries with it several strategic and economic disadvantages including lack of control, and questionable long-term cost stability.

C: New Metal Fabrication System

This alternative replaces existing equipment with newer technology. Among the principal benefits are reduced labor, inventories and material handling. The new machine tools do not require continuous operator attendance, and flexibility and response time are improved significantly.

The new equipment can operate unattended through coffee breaks, lunch periods, and shift changes. Both the operator and machine tools operate independently of each other because of appropriate job queuing. The operator to machine ratio is also reduced.

Raw material, work in process, and finished goods inventories are minimized because **set-up time is greatly reduced**, and all of the work required on the parts is done, basically in one continuous sequence of operations, (except forming) including manual deburring operations. Raw sheet material goes in, and flat parts come out in one continuous process. Lead time is greatly reduced and there are a limited number of partially completed parts (work in process) on the shop floor.

Comparison Of Alternatives
(Based On Two Shift Operation)

Alternative	A	B	C
Item Description	Present System	Farm Out	New System
Number of machines	4	N/A	3
Number of people required	6	N/A	4
Hours per year per machine	4,000	N/A	4,000
Total hours available per year	16,000	N/A	8,000
Average equipment utilization	75%	N/A	90%
Net metal cutting hours per year	12,000	12,000	10,800
Set up hours per year	2,000	N/A	800
Operator cost per hour	$20.00	N/A	$20.00
Hours per year per operator	2,000	N/A	2,000
Labor cost per year	$240,000	$600,000	$160,000
Cost per metal cutting hour	$20.00	$50.00	$14.81
Annual savings:	None	($360,000)	**$80,000**
Raw Material			
Annual cost	$2,000,000	$2,000,000	$1,600,000
Annual savings:	None	None	**$400,000**
Material Handling			
Annual cost	$15,000	$0	$10,000
Annual savings:	None	$15,000	**$5,000**
Inventories			
Inventory turns per year	10	20	50
Average inventory value	$25,000	$12,500	$5,000
One time inventory reduction	None	$12,500	**$20,000**
Carrying costs @ 10%	$2,500	$1,250	$500
Annual savings:	None	$1,250	**$2,000**
Total annual savings:	None	($343,750)	**$487,000**

Conclusion And Recommendation

Proceed with the implementation of alternative C, the new metal fabrication system, and recover the benefits as outlined.

Metal Fabrication System
Discounted Cash Flow Summary

Item Description	Time Now	Year 1	Year 2	Year 3	Year 4	Year 5
Program Costs						
Equipment	$1,250,000					
Tooling	$100,000					
Expenses	$150,000					
Total:	$1,500,000					
Cash Flows						
Depreciation		$283,000	$444,000	$260,500	$187,500	$175,000
Reduced Inventories		15,000	5,000			
Residual Value of Equipment						250,000
Annual Savings		250,000	487,000	487,000	487,000	487,000
Taxes	38%	95,000	185,060	185,060	185,060	185,060
Tax Credit	10%	N/A				
After Tax Earnings						
Future Values		$453,000	$750,940	$562,440	$489,440	$726,940
Discount Rate Per Year		5.0%				
Present Values		$431,430	$681,127	$485,860	$402,667	$569,581
Program Summary (After Tax)						
Net Present Value		$1,070,664				
Internal Rate Of Return		21.1%				
Payback Period (Years)		2.8				

Table reflects 1995 data, however 2025 would be 70% to 75% higher due to inflation.

Cost of materials, labor, and equipment will have increased accordingly, however this would have little impact on the program justification itself.

Robot Welding System
(Proposal)

July 4, 1995
Tim Fleskes

Program Title: **Robot Welding System**

Reference Number: (Fill this in as needed)

Program Amount: **$750,000**

Synopsis:

Recent developments in robot welding systems and technology offer the opportunity to greatly improve and upgrade our own in-house welding operations. This newer technology is **proven** and currently used in several manufacturing facilities throughout the country.

The proposal outlines a new robot welding system for our applications, which will result in higher productivity, lower inventories, faster response time, better quality, and reduced product cost.

The strategic and economic advantages are significant. Based on two shift utilization of the proposed system, the projected annual savings of **$162,000** per year and other cash flow benefits generate an **after tax** annual internal return on investment of **15.1%** with a net present value of **$352,387** and payback period of **3.1** years.

Background:

Our present manual welding operations include equipment, technology and fixtures which have been in service for many years, and have successfully provided the required product quality and thruput. However, the opportunity to greatly improve our welding productivity and product consistency is apparent, and readily achievable.

Currently our welding operations are very labor intensive. The welders must load the fixtures, weld the parts, then remove the weldments from the fixtures. Changes required in the weld schedules or position of the weldment must be made manually by the operator to accommodate varying weld requirements.

Average arc-on time for the current welding systems is approximately 25 to 30% of the total time for the job, so utilization of the welding equipment is correspondingly low.

Robot Welding System Proposal

Alternatives:

Three basic alternatives are presented for your consideration:

A: Present System (Do nothing)

Doing nothing is the easiest, but nothing will improve. Manufacturing costs will continue to increase, not decrease. Product consistency and quality will continue to be difficult to maintain, and thruput will be limited to what can be produced with the current equipment and technology on hand.

B: Farm Out

Welding operations can be farmed out or out-sourced to sub-contractors, but at a significant cost premium, as will be seen in the following summaries. This alternative carries with it several strategic and economic disadvantages including lack of control, and questionable long-term cost stability.

C: New Robot Welding System

This alternative replaces existing equipment with newer technology using computer-controlled welding robots and positioners. Among the principal benefits are reduced labor and inventories. Average arc-on time is expected to double from the current 25 to 30% range, to 50 to 60%, or even higher with the new robot welding systems.

Weld settings, procedures, and sequences, are highly repeatable, and flexibility and response time are improved significantly. For example, weld voltage, current, and wire feed and torch travel speed settings can be adjusted under program control to accommodate different weldment configurations and requirements.

The system consists of two welding robots, with four positioners. A new family of welding fixtures designed for robot welding is planned, and included in the proposal. Funds are also included for improving the manufacturing repeatability of several of the parts required for the weldments.

The welding robots can operate unattended for short periods of time, through coffee breaks, lunch periods, and shift changes to the extent that fixtures and parts can be queued in advance. The system operator and the welding robot operate independently of each other because of appropriate job queuing using multiple fixture pallets.

Comparison Of Alternatives
(Based On Two Shift Operation)

Alternative	A	B	C
Item Description	Present System	Farm Out	New System
Number of machines	4	N/A	2
Number of people required	8	N/A	4
Hours per year per machine	4,000	N/A	4,000
Total hours available per year	16,000	N/A	8,000
Average equipment utilization	90%	N/A	90%
Net hours welding per year	14,400	14,400	7,200
Arc on-time percent	25%	N/A	50%
Annual arc-on hours	3,600	N/A	3,600
Set up hours per year	500	N/A	500
Operator cost per hour	$20.00	N/A	$20.00
Hours per year per operator	2,000	N/A	2,000
Labor cost per year	$320,000	$720,000	$160,000
Cost per fabrication hour	$88.89	$50.00	$44.44
Annual savings:		($400,000)	**$160,000**
Inventories			
Inventory turns per year	10	20	50
Average inventory value	$25,000	$12,500	$5,000
One time inventory reduction	None	$12,500	**$20,000**
Carrying costs @ 10%	$2,500	$1,250	$500
Annual savings:	None	$1,250	**$2,000**
Total annual savings:	None	($397,500)	**$162,000**

Conclusion And Recommendation

Proceed with the implementation of alternative C, the new robot welding system, and recover the benefits as outlined.

Robot Welding System
Discounted Cash Flow Summary

Item Description	Time Now	Year 1	Year 2	Year 3	Year 4	Year 5
Program Costs						
Equipment	$500,000					
Fixtures	$175,000					
Expenses	$75,000					
Total:	$750,000					
Cash Flows						
Depreciation		$157,750	$237,000	$135,250	$75,000	$70,000
Reduced Inventories		15,000	5,000			
Residual Value of Equipment						125,000
Annual Savings		81,000	182,000	182,000	182,000	182,000
Taxes	38%	30,780	61,560	61,560	61,560	61,560
Tax Credit	10%	N/A				
After Tax Earnings						
Future Values		$222,970	$342,440	$235,690	$175,440	$295,440
Discount Rate Per Year		5.0%				
Present Values		$212,353	$310,605	$203,601	$144,338	$231,489
Program Summary (After Tax)						
Net Present Value		$352,387				
Internal Rate Of Return		15.1%				
Payback Period (Years)		3.1				

Table reflects 1995 data, however 2025 would be 70% to 75% higher due to inflation.

Cost of materials, labor, and equipment will have increased accordingly, however, this would have little impact on the program justification itself.

Computer Support System
(Proposal)

July 4, 1995
Tim Fleskes

Synopsis:

Recent developments in manufacturing require information, lots of it, to operate the various types of new machinery. This newer Computer Integrated Manufacturing (CIM) technology is proven, and currently used in several manufacturing facilities throughout the country.

The benefits of this technology are staggering.

Think of it . . . error free manufacturing of parts and assemblies. No mistakes. No scrap. Minimal set up time. Unattended equipment operations. Machines running through coffee breaks, lunches, and shift changes. Higher productivity and thruput. Lower inventories. Faster response time. Better quality. Reduced product cost. And more . . .

But it requires information, (lots of it), and it **must** be error free. Computers are very good at doing this job, and they are much better at it than people.

Background:

Present manual manufacturing operations include equipment technology and fixtures which have been in service for many years, and have successfully provided the required product quality and thruput. However, the opportunity to substantially improve our productivity and technology is readily apparent, obvious, and currently available, as computer supported and integrated manufacturing systems.

Currently, machine operators must load parts into the fixtures, start the machine cycle, then wait, or find something else to do, such as deburring or inspecting parts, while the machine works on the parts. When the machine is finished, then the operator must remove the parts from the fixtures, and the machine has to wait. What a vicious circle.

Utilization of the operator and the machinery are both compromised severely because neither can get their work done without forcing the other to wait. Rarely do they balance each other very well.

Computer Support System Proposal

Alternatives:

Two basic alternatives are presented for your consideration:

A: Present System (Do nothing)

Doing nothing is the easiest. But, nothing will improve. Manufacturing costs will continue to increase, not decrease.

B: Install New Computer Support Systems

This alternative provides the computer hardware and software required to support the manufacturing system. The principal benefits have already been mentioned.

But, beware of overkill.

Concentrate on what the system needs, to work the way it should, and provide that. Don't get burned with an overly sophisticated system that few can understand, and nobody can make work.

Comparison of Alternatives

There is little room for comparisons here. The computers and software are a fact of life if we expect to be competitive in the marketplace. It simply must be done to stay in business.

Conclusion and Recommendation

Proceed with the implementation of the new computer support system, and recover the benefits.

If you're looking for return on investment, payback, net present value, and annual savings for justification, then look to the project analyses that the computer system is designed to support. If these analysis can't justify this additional expense, then maybe the project(s) should be reconsidered.

10

Finally . . .
Go On From Here

Acknowledge the skills of all those who have gone before us in implementing the manufacturing systems that are presently in place. It took (I am sure) considerable effort on their part to get us where we are. We must be grateful, and they must be respected for their contributions.

Finally, Go On From Here . . .

In this next to last chapter, I want to leave you with a message and a challenge to go on from here, to implement change. To make change a part of your business life and an idea that permeates throughout your organization . . .

If you plant the seed, and nurture it, it will grow.

Unleashing Your Productivity.

It is not finished with reading this book, it is only the beginning.

Here are some things to think about and do:

> Use **UNLEASHING PRODUCTIVITY** as a tool and/or guide to enhance and improve productivity in your own organization.
>
> Be willing to take a risk to make things better.
>
> Be more competitive . . . than your competition.
>
> Challenge yourself . . . and meet the challenge.
>
> Make improving productivity a strategic objective.
>
> Look for the opportunities to make things better.
>
> Make productivity improvement ideas work.
>
> Find a champion, and let them spirit the cause.
>
> Challenge the status quo. Get some different ideas.
>
> Convince your board of directors and executive committee that there is more to corporate life than next quarter's earnings.
>
> Accept the responsibility to improve, and make it happen.

Rewards and Benefits

Budget future capital requirements with a rolling five-year plan with emphasis on the near term for productivity improvement expenditures.

Look at examples of how others have done it.

All it takes is a lot of commitment, some money, and someone to make it happen.

Develop a long-term strategy, and a long-term plan.

Start from where you are, and build a better tomorrow.

Your rewards (among other things) are stronger market position, better product quality, lower product costs, and improved long term earnings.

If you don't do it, your competition will.

Believe that you can do it too.

The possibilities are endless.

Look around you: It's there.

Just do it.

Rewards and Benefits for the Organization

Some reasons why . . .

- Better quality
- Lower labor costs
- Lower material costs
- Greater flexibility

More reasons why . . .

    Less scrap

    Higher yield

    Lower lead times

    Fewer or no set ups

    Less floor space required

    Lower equipment maintenance costs

    Fewer manufacturing operations

    Lower overall fixture costs

    Less job specific tooling

    Less material handling

    Faster product thruput

    Less manual intervention

    Higher equipment utilization

    Equipment operates unattended

    Reduced outside expenses

    Quicker response time

    Reduced or no paperwork

    More predictable product costs

Increased Demands on the Organization

Some reasons why it's hard . . .

    It takes time

    It takes money

    Personnel training

    Personnel re-training

    Personnel re-assignment

    Must do a better job of planning

    Must involve people in the changes

    Must learn and absorb new technology

    Must work closer with suppliers and customers

    Need to plan to provide increased amounts of capital funds

    Must give up old faithful (reliance on personal notes, etc.)

    Be willing to accept and want to change

    Must learn to communicate better

    Must become computer literate

    Must give up old faithful

    Must try harder

11

Not Where To Be . . .

*Unleash
Your
Productivity*

Chapter Eleven . . .

This is **not** where you want or need to be.

There is just no reason to be here.

In case you didn't recognize it,
this is the first step into receivership and bankruptcy.

But, if you accept and make the ongoing commitment to

UNLEASHING PRODUCTIVITY

there is no need, nor likelihood, you will ever find yourself in

"Chapter Eleven"

Wishing you good luck, and good business,

Tim Fleskes

Tim Fleskes

This is the all there is of chapter eleven.

And, this is the end of the book.

Appendices

Appendix A – Summary of Charts And Graphs

Item	Page
United States Foreign Trade	7
Annual Productivity Growth Rate	9
Self-Test	11
Make Or Buy Analysis Summary	25
Make Or Buy Comparison	26
Project Anatomy	31
Data Matrix (Horizontal Machining Center Comparison)	63
Discounted Cash Flow Summary (Basic Example)	79
Metal Removal System	127
Metal Fabrication System	133
Robot Welding System	139
Project Format Outline	87
Project Implementation Schedule	103
Cumulative Cash Flow (Typical Project)	119
Comparison Of Alternatives	
Metal Removal System	126
Metal Fabrication System	132
Robot Welding System	138

Appendix B – Axioms and Food for Thought

A substantial part, or even all of the funds required to implement improvements in productivity may in fact be directly recoverable from reductions in inventories, and inventory maintenance costs alone.

Eliminating opportunities for manual intervention in the production cycle will result in significant reductions in product costs and improved quality.

Involving the people in change, and inviting their input and participation during the developmental and start up phases of a project will virtually assure a successful implementation of a good productivity improvement idea.

Be kind to manufacturing engineers.

The potential residual value of assets are frequently overlooked, or not even used in the financial justification phase of a project. They should be.

Engineering the cost of materials and/or labor operations out of the product without compromising product functionality and customer acceptance is the surest and easiest way to reduce product costs.

Additional opportunities can be found in reviewing the initial engineering design to search for potential material savings and ease of manufacturing. This cannot be overemphasized! Always look, and then look again.

Effective utilization of resources is the key to achieving acceptable return on investment and optimizing payback period. Not Minimizing Investment.

Keeping a project journal where relevant activity can be recorded chronologically is a valuable reference tool.

Personal or informational credibility and integrity **must never be compromised**. Your success is entirely dependent on doing what you say you will do when you say you will do it. Always keep appropriate parties advised of significant and relevant open issues related to the project, especially events which may delay the implementation.

More axioms and food for thought . . .

Listening is probably the most intelligent thing we can do. We have two ears and one mouth which is most indicative of the importance of developing this skill as opposed to speaking. It's doubtful that anyone has achieved anything without practicing and developing their listening skills to a significant degree.

Try communicating without listening . . . it doesn't work very well.

On the importance of effective communications . . . **Critical**.

Cost avoidance should be considered in discounted cash flow calculations as potential positive cash flows.

Acknowledge the skills of all those who have gone before us in implementing the manufacturing systems that are presently in place. It took, I am sure, considerable effort on their part to get us where we are. We must be grateful, and they must be respected for their contributions.

The entrepreneurial spirit, commitment to excellence, and the motivation to do what it takes to make things better are frequently lost, or greatly reduced when remote ownership controls the organizational strategy. The willingness to make things better and take the calculated risk becomes more obscure. The short-term earnings motive takes over, and cripples the organization's propensity for making funds available for improvement programs.

Do what needs to be done as soon as you possibly can. You'll find you will get a lot more done, and people will be surprised at how much you accomplish.

Machines and robots do not need personal, fatigue, and delay allowances (P,F & D).

Let machines do what machines do best.

Let people do what people do best.

and . . . **Don't let them get in each other's way**.

Appendix C – Abbreviations, Acronyms and Definitions

ABC	Activity Based Costing
	A system of allocating cost to a product or process based on activities which directly contribute value to the product or service, whether they are proportional to direct labor or not.
	Also refers to system of classification, or grouping of items, such as inventories, based on value or other attributes.
Actual Cost	Our best shot at determining the real direct and indirect cash flows and allocations (dollars) related to a product or manufacturing process from documentation such as invoices and work order history evaluation and analysis.
AGV	Automatic Guided Vehicle
AI	Artificial Intelligence
Alternative	Other possible, realistic and viable ways of achieving the same or better end results.
Amortization	A system or allocation method designed to distribute a one-time cost or expense over a period of time, or product quantity.
APT	Automatically Programmed Tool (path) Numerical control programming language.
ASRS	Automatic Storage and Retrieval System
Attrition	Allowing a reduction in labor force to occur over a period of time from normal causes such as employee turnover, or retirement.
Avoidance	Eliminating the potential for a future expenditure. (See cost avoidance)
AWGV	Automatic Wire Guided Vehicle
Benefit Analysis	A summary of benefits or advantages and disadvantages

BOM or B/M	Bill of Materials, or list of items and quantities required to construct a part or assembly
Bottleneck	A manufacturing operation whose thruput rate limits both subsequent and previous operation thruput rates
Burden	A cost, usually based on actual expenses, applied to a product or service, according to an arbitrary allocation formula, designed to recover actual expenses. An example would be $35.00 per direct labor hour, to recover indirect costs such as vacations, medical insurance, rent, the electric bill, and so forth.
CAD	Computer Aided Design
CAE	Computer Aided Engineering
CAM	Computer Aided Manufacturing
Capacity	The amount of product that can be reasonably expected to be cycled through a manufacturing operation for a given period of time and a given quantity of resources. (See thruput.) Also, may refer to the maximum capability of a machine, in terms of tonnage as with a punch press, or spindle horsepower or torque as with a machining center.
Capital	The funds required for a project to purchase and install machinery and equipment, which will be booked as an asset for the company, and depreciated in accordance with federal regulations.
Carrying Cost	The costs associated with maintaining inventories, including allowances for the space, handling, tracking, managing, insuring, and financing the inventory. A conservative number typically used is 10% of the value of the inventory.
Cash Flow	Refers to the movement of cash in, and out, of the organization related to a specific issue. Usually refers to external cash flows, which exclude internal cash flows such as depreciation
Cell	A group of machines which operate as a unit in generating thruput for the organization
CIFM	Computer Integrated Flexible Manufacturing

CIM	Computer Integrated Manufacturing. A manufacturing system which is scheduled, controlled and monitored using computers
CMM	Co-ordinate Measuring Machine
CNC	Computer Numerical Control. Usually refers to the type of controller used on a machine. A computer-controlled machine.
Confidence Level	Refers to the reliability (CREDIBILITY) of the information being provided.
Consumable	Expensed materials and supplies used in the manufacturing processes, which in themselves are relatively minor, but over the long haul, may add up to a significant amount of money. Examples are cleaning solvents, rags, industrial gases, welding wire, etc.
Cost Avoidance	Being able to state that an expense or expenditure would necessarily **not** occur if a particular option or alternative were selected. An example would be avoiding the cost of major maintenance expense on a machine that would be replaced with new equipment.
Cost-Benefit Ratio	A method of expressing and comparing the relative worth of different investment opportunities.
Credibility	**Pay attention to this one.** Whether your proposals are accepted or not may be based **entirely** on the integrity of the proposal, and your **credibility**.

Do not compromise under any circumstances. |
Data Matrix	A spreadsheet or information table.
D&B	Dunn and Bradstreet. An institution providing analyses and/or financial information about a business.
DCF	See Discounted Cash Flow.
Demand	Refers to the entire market for your product or service. Your product and service sales only represent your market share of the total demand.

Depreciation	A non-cash-out expense, booked monthly on the profit and loss statement (which effectively reduces the Business Tax Liability). Depreciation is designed to recover funds expended for capital equipment.
DEQ	Department Of Environmental Quality.
Direct Cost	By definition, those costs that can only be directly associated with the product or service. Don't muddy the water here. Verify and confirm every penny.
Direct Labor Rate	The rate usually established as an average for the shop. It should not be used in project analysis because it usually covers payroll issues only and will not necessarily apply directly to the project. For example, it probably does not include allowances for vacations, medical care, or employer paid social security etc. The direct labor rate is not the same as the incremental direct cost of labor.
Discount	A potential reduction in amount payable on an invoice, if paid within a specified period of time. Your company may or may not be taking advantage of these discounts, depending on their cash flow situation.
Discounted Cash Flow	A mathematical procedure that reduces the value of future cash flows to current dollars at a predetermined discount rate to help compare and evaluate the benefits of alternative programs.
DNC	Direct Numerical Control. Refers to a communications capability, or link, between support computers and machinery or equipment. Used extensively in computer integrated manufacturing systems.
Earnings	The funds adding to the net value of the business at the end of the accounting period, which usually consist of profit after taxes plus depreciation. Net earnings may also be significantly affected by the sale of assets, or other income and expenses.
EPA	Environmental Protection Agency.
Equipment	Facilities, machinery, fixtures, tooling as needed, etc.
Facilities	Buildings and support equipment such as compressors, chillers, electrical service, etc.

Farm-out	Having work done by outside contractors that cannot get done in-house (outsource). This may or may not be justified, but it probably costs more to have it done outside than do it in-house if the capacity already exists to get the job done.
FFS	Flexible Fabrication System.
FIFO	First In First Out.
Finished Goods	Inventories that are finished and ready to ship to the customer or user.
Fixed Cost	An expenditure that can be allocated into product cost, based on a ratio reflecting the use of that resource.
Fixture	Device built to hold work-pieces.
FMC	Flexible Manufacturing Cell.
FMS	Flexible Manufacturing System.
FOB	Freight On Board. Equipment packed, ready for shipment, and loaded onto the carrier. Usually at the source location.
Fringe Benefit	Usually refers to benefits provided for employees such as vacations, holidays, medical care, sick leave, etc.
Fully Burdened Cost	A cost that includes all allocations of direct and indirect expenses, such as direct labor, allowances for depreciation, supervision, janitorial, material handling, etc.
Future Value	A term used to distinguish between present funds in today's dollars, and the value of those funds at some future date.
G-CODE	A set of instructions sent to Machine Tools (e.g. Part programs), or Programmable Logic Controllers (PLC's), to tell it what to do and when, and sometimes other data as well.
Gauge	An instrument or tool used in lieu of a measuring device. For example a plug or pin gauge for verifying a hole diameter. Gauges can get quite complex, but are much faster than using a measuring device. Remember, they do not add any value to the product, only confirm or verify a pre-existing condition.
GD&T	Geometric Dimensions and Tolerances

GIGO	Garbage In Garbage Out (Your results are only as good as the information given) Bad information usually ends up with bad results.
Graphic	A picture, diagram, or illustration (Are they really worth a thousand words?)
GT-Group Technology	A grouping of similar parts which use common processes, fixtures, and/or tools in manufacturing. Significant economies of scale can be achieved when product variables can be accommodated automatically.
Hurdle Rate	An interest rate or internal rate of return (IRR) for a program, below which the project will not be considered for implementation without very significant other influences. Can be a fairly arbitrary number.
Incremental	That additional investment or benefit resulting from further analysis and consideration of other issues. (Marginal)
Indirect Cost	A cost that cannot or is not directly allocated to the product.
Internal cost of capital	The interest expense imposed on the organization associated with borrowing additional capital funds.
Internal Rate Of Return	The interest rate associated with the periodic cash flows for a specific project. (IRR)
Investment	All the funds required to implement a program, usually includes capital as well as non-capital expenditures.
Investment Tax Credit (ITC)	A tax credit periodically and/or selectively authorized by congress designed to encourage capital investment.
Justification	The benefits associated with implementation of a specific project. The most common terms are annual savings, net present value, internal rate of return, and payback period.
Labor	The manual effort required to add value to the product.
LAN	Local Area Network. A data communications system to allow various devices (equipment) to communicate with computers and each other.
LIFO	Last In First Out.

Literacy	As in **Computer literacy**. A must capability for present and future employees. We are in the computer communications age.
MAP	Manufacturing Automation Protocol. A set of ground rules for data communications designed to allow equipment and machine controllers from different manufacturers to talk to each other.
Marginal	Borderline, a close call, almost there, an increment away.
MIL-TDD41	Make It Like The Damn Drawing For Once.
MRP	Material Requirements Planning
MRP-II	More sophisticated MRP
MTBF	Mean (Average) Time Between Failure.
Non-Taxable Income	Revenue or income not subject to tax (Depreciation)
NPV	Net Present Value. The amount of funds in today's dollars, in excess of those required to generate the periodic cash flow pattern consistent with the project under consideration.
OSHA	Occupational Safety and Health Administration
Out-source	See farm-out
Overhead	Indirect expenses associated with manufacturing operations. Usually allocated to the product by establishing a rate to apply to product costing that will result in recovery of indirect expenses.
P&L	Profit and Loss (Statement)
Payback	Payback period. The amount of time required to recover the investment for a project. Usually expressed in months or years.
PF&D	Personal, Fatigue, and Delay allowances. Not allowed for machine tools and robots.
PIP	Productivity Improvement Project, Potential, or Profile

PLC	Programmable Logic Controller. An industrial grade machine controller that can be programmed for specific applications, such as control of processes and machines.
Premium	An additional amount of funds, over and above a basic amount, that may be required for, or to encourage specific performance. As in shortening delivery time on a piece of equipment, or the overtime portion of a rate paid a sub-contractor to meet delivery commitments.
Present Value	Funds expressed in today's dollars. (PV) See Future Value.
Productivity	A ratio of thruput to resources utilized. See thruput.
Project Term	The length of time over which a program is evaluated. Usually three, five, seven or ten years, depending on the estimated life of the capital assets.
Queue	A position, or material provided in the manufacturing system to allow the next work piece to be immediately available, so that production delays are minimized or eliminated.
Remote Ownership	A scenario where the business owners are not located at the business site, and may have limited knowledge about the operations of the business and it's needs.
Residual Value	The value of the manufacturing system or equipment at the end of the project term.
RFP	Request For Proposal
RFQ	Request For Quotation
ROI	Return On Investment
Set-up	The time required to get ready to do the job. As in setting up the machine, fixtures and tools to do the work. This is necessary, but should be minimized as much as possible, without compromising thruput potential or quality.
SPCME	Society for the Prevention of Cruelty to Manufacturing Engineers.

Stand-Alone	A manufacturing scenario which places an operator at each machine, very common in present manufacturing systems, and results in considerable imbalance in operator and machine utilization, and therefore reduced productivity.
STEP	A manufacturing time or cost that the product is expected to require to produce it.
Standard	A standard for the exchange of Product Data, and is commonly used for sharing 3D model data between CAD Systems
Strategy	A plan. Have at least one, several is better
Sunk	Usually refers to an amount of funds that have been expended and are not recoverable
Taxable Income	Most revenues in excess of expenses
Thruput	A quantity of products or services over a period of time. **Think of Thruput as finished product out the door, and shipped to the customer.** If it's not out the door, it isn't finished, and it's not thruput.
TLC	Tender Loving Care. What machine tools, robots, fixtures, tooling and manufacturing engineers need most.
Tooling	Devices that actually contact the material to remove the metal or change its shape. For example, punches and dies for piercing and/or forming, drill bits, and milling cutters.
Utilization	How much, how well, or how effectively a resource, whether material, equipment, or labor is used.
Value Added	Changing the shape, properties, or appearance of material will add value to the product. This is what determines the cost of the product. No value is added when parts are moved internally in the organization or when they are inspected.
Variable Cost	A cost which directly relates to the product configuration. For example, material, machine time, and labor.
WGV	Wire Guided Vehicle

WIP	Work in Process or Progress (inventory). Products that are partially completed. Avoid this as much as possible.
WYSIWYG	What You See Is What You Get. (User friendly display.)
WYSINWYG	What You See Is Not What You Get. (Not so user friendly.)

Index

A

Accuracy, 64, 75
Acquisition, 30, 101, 112
Acronyms, 161
Activity Based Costing, 161
Actual Cost, 50, 51, 161
Allocation, 47, 49, 57, 59, 73, 74, 161, 162
Alternative, 5, 6, 20, 22, 32, 61, 62, 77, 78, 85, 91, 113, 125, 126, 131, 132, 137, 138, 143, 161, 163, 164
Amortization, 50, 54, 73, 74, 161
Analysis, 25, 28, 36, 46, 47, 48, 52, 54, 57, 58, 59, 60, 62, 65, 67, 72, 78, 80, 81, 84, 87, 96, 102, 157
Arrangement, 86, 108, 112
Asset, 16, 56, 70, 73, 81, 96, 121, 162, 164, 168
Attrition, 161
Audit, 103, 117
Automation, 5, 10, 113
Avoidance, 81, 161
Axioms, 159, 160

B

Balance Sheet, 16, 51, 78
Benefit, 11, 12, 18, 20, 24, 25, 27, 28, 36, 46, 47, 50, 53, 74, 76, 98, 99, 118, 122, 126, 132, 138, 142, 143, 147, 161, 162, 164, 165, 166, 167
Benefit Analysis, 28, 162
Bid, 22, 87, 111
Bottleneck, 24, 162
Budget, 27, 28, 30, 70, 96, 114, 147
Burden, 23, 47, 49, 51, 58, 162

C

Capacity, 22, 24, 38, 65, 67, 80, 88, 89, 165
Capital, 4, 6, 10, 22, 23, 24, 25, 27, 28, 33, 36, 41, 46, 53, 54, 70, 71, 72, 75, 78, 98, 114, 118, 147, 149, 164, 166, 168
Capital Plan, 27
Carrying Cost, 162
Cash Flow, 24, 29, 50, 53, 78, 79, 85, 99, 118, 119, 124, 127, 130, 133, 136, 139, 157, 160, 161, 162, 164
Chief Executive Officer, 163
Commitment, 1, 4, 13, 30, 43, 54, 70, 71, 122, 147, 152, 160
Comparison, 22, 25, 28, 87, 126, 132, 138, 143, 157
Computer Aided Design, 162
Computer Aided Engineering, 162
Computer Aided Manufacturing, 162
Computer Integrated Manufacturing, 10, 74, 142, 163, 164
Computer Numerical Control, 163
Concept, 8, 27, 28, 40, 89
Confidence Level, 116, 163
Consumable, 60, 163
Contribution, 23, 27, 30, 38, 57, 74, 78
Cost, 6, 10, 16, 17, 21, 22, 23, 24, 25, 28, 46, 47, 48, 49, 50, 51, 52, 53, 54, 56, 57, 58, 59, 60, 61, 65, 67, 74, 77, 78, 80, 81, 87, 89, 98, 99, 104, 107, 114, 124, 125, 126, 130, 131, 132, 136, 137, 142, 160, 161, 162, 163, 165, 166, 169, 170
Cost Avoidance, 160, 163
Cost of Capital, 16, 166
Cost-Benefit Ratio, 163
Credibility, 30, 46, 47, 48, 52, 83, 84, 87, 89, 90, 92, 96, 98, 102, 117, 159, 163

Customer, 16, 19, 24, 40, 42, 43, 54, 74, 85, 99, 116, 169

D

Data Matrix, 61, 62, 63, 64, 77, 157, 163
Demand, 5, 22, 24, 25, 41, 42, 61, 66, 67, 97, 164
Department Of Environmental Quality, 164
Depreciation, 24, 25, 33, 47, 50, 54, 71, 72, 73, 74, 78, 79, 81, 127, 133, 139, 162, 164, 165, 167
Depreciation Schedule, 71, 73, 164
Direct Cost, 164
Direct Numerical Control, 164
Discount, 79, 127, 133, 139, 164
Discounted Cash Flow, 28, 46, 62, 72, 78, 79, 80, 81, 87, 127, 160, 163, 164

E

Earnings, 4, 11, 13, 71, 72, 79, 127, 133, 139, 146, 147, 160, 164
Economic, 1, 8, 12, 13, 27, 33, 37, 46, 47, 49, 50, 67, 72, 77, 85, 87, 124, 125, 130, 131, 136, 137
Environment, 12, 18, 37, 39, 74, 104
Environmental Protection Agency, 164
Equipment, 11, 12, 16, 22, 23, 24, 25, 28, 30, 32, 33, 38, 39, 41, 46, 53, 54, 55, 57, 62, 64, 65, 67, 71, 72, 73, 74, 75, 76, 78, 79, 80, 85, 87, 101, 108, 110, 111, 112, 114, 115, 116, 118, 124, 125, 126, 130, 131, 132, 136, 137, 138, 142, 148, 162, 163, 164, 165, 167, 168, 169
Equipment Replacement, 32, 71, 80
Error, 142
Evaluation, 28, 29, 30, 36, 77, 161
Expense, 16, 17, 46, 49, 60, 67, 71, 73, 74, 143, 161, 163, 164, 166

F

Facilities, 53, 72, 101, 108, 124, 130, 136, 142
Farm Out, 24, 25, 125, 131, 137

Finance, 19, 28, 53, 91
Finished Goods, 124, 125, 130, 131, 165
Fixed, 30, 41, 49, 55, 61, 67, 117
Fixed Cost, 49, 165

G

Gauge, 165
Graphic, 86, 90, 166
Group Technology, 166

H

Hazardous, 39
Hurdle Rate, 78, 80, 166

I

Idea, 12, 15, 27, 28, 33, 37, 48, 70, 72, 110, 146, 159
Image, 38, 43, 85, 99
Improvement, 8, 11, 12, 13, 15, 16, 17, 18, 25, 27, 28, 33, 36, 37, 38, 39, 41, 42, 46, 48, 50, 53, 58, 67, 70, 72, 75, 76, 77, 89, 146, 147, 159, 160
Incentive, 38
Incremental, 49, 78, 164, 166
Index, 171
Indirect Cost, 49, 166
Inflation, 46
Inspection, 41, 55
Installation, 39, 54, 72, 103, 108, 114, 115
Intangible, 85
Integrity, 24, 40, 41, 47, 73, 83, 96, 101, 159, 163
Internal Rate of Return, 166, 167
Internal Rate Of Return, 79, 127, 133, 139, 166
International Graphics Exchange Specification, 166
Inventory, 3, 16, 50, 65, 78, 81, 99, 126, 132, 138, 159, 162, 170
Investment, 6, 10, 22, 23, 25, 36, 45, 54, 69, 71, 72, 73, 78, 80, 98, 118, 163, 166, 168
Investment Tax Credit, 72, 79, 166

J

Justification, 67, 121, 143, 167

L

Labor, 5, 6, 8, 10, 16, 22, 23, 33, 46, 47, 49, 50, 51, 52, 57, 65, 99, 125, 131, 136, 137, 147, 161, 162, 164, 165, 169, 170
Legal, 19
Literacy, 76, 167
Local Area Network, 167
Loss, 73

M

Machinery, 142, 162, 164
Maintenance, 3, 5, 19, 24, 30, 32, 39, 56, 65, 70, 74, 75, 76, 80, 81, 87, 89, 99, 103, 114, 115, 125, 131, 148, 159, 163
Manual, 5, 10, 23, 42, 69, 113, 116, 125, 131, 136, 142, 148, 159, 167
Manufacturing, 1, 4, 5, 6, 8, 10, 11, 13, 16, 19, 20, 21, 22, 23, 24, 25, 27, 32, 37, 39, 40, 41, 42, 43, 48, 49, 50, 51, 52, 58, 66, 70, 74, 75, 89, 104, 113, 114, 118, 122, 124, 130, 136, 137, 142, 143, 145, 148, 159, 160, 161, 162, 163, 166, 168, 169
Manufacturing Automation Protocol, 167
Marginal, 40, 80, 166, 167
Mark Up, 50
Material Flow, 37, 42, 58
Material Handling, 19, 58, 81, 99, 125, 126, 131, 132, 148, 165
Material Requirements Planning, 167
Medical, 47, 162, 164, 165
Motivation, 5, 18, 38, 160

N

Net Present Value, 72, 78, 79, 80, 124, 127, 130, 133, 136, 139, 143, 167
Network, 40
Non-Quantifiable, 28, 36, 37, 80, 85, 87
Non-Taxable Income, 164, 167

O

Occupational Safety and Health Act, 39
Occupational Safety And Health Act, 167
Out-source, 167
Overhead, 8, 23, 25, 33, 47, 49, 50, 51, 58, 65, 168

P

Payback Period, 45, 53, 72, 78, 79, 98, 118, 124, 127, 130, 133, 136, 139, 159, 167, 168
Performance, 40, 50, 57, 96, 116, 117, 122, 168
Personal Computer, 74, 168
Perspective, 5, 6, 18, 25, 37, 75, 80, 97
Premium, 125, 131, 137, 168
Present Value, 168
Process, 18, 20, 21, 23, 24, 27, 30, 36, 37, 48, 52, 54, 57, 58, 59, 60, 67, 77, 89, 91, 96, 97, 125, 131, 161
Productivity, 1, 3, 4, 5, 6, 8, 9, 10, 11, 12, 13, 15, 16, 17, 18, 19, 27, 28, 33, 36, 37, 38, 39, 41, 42, 46, 48, 50, 53, 58, 65, 66, 67, 70, 72, 75, 76, 104, 114, 122, 124, 130, 136, 142, 146, 147, 151, 157, 159, 168, 169
Productivity Improvement Potential, 168
Productivity Improvement Profile, 168
Profit, 20, 23, 24, 38, 71, 164
Profit and Loss, 16, 48, 78, 164, 168
Programmable Logic Controller, 75, 168
Programming, 5, 74, 116, 161
Project Term, 80, 168
Purchasing, 19, 52, 101, 110

Q

Quality, 1, 19, 21, 23, 24, 30, 32, 33, 37, 38, 40, 41, 43, 55, 58, 69, 85, 87, 89, 98, 124, 125, 130, 131, 136, 137, 142, 147, 159
Quantifiable, 33, 35, 45
Quantity, 8, 59, 67, 161, 162, 169
Queue, 168
Quotation, 64

173

R

Raw Materials, 48, 58, 59, 67, 130
Reduction, 67, 126, 132, 138, 161, 164
Remote Ownership, 4, 160, 168
Repeatability, 137
Request For Proposal, 168
Request For Quotation, 169
Research, 41, 70, 96
Residual Value, 78, 79, 80, 121, 127, 133, 139, 168
Return On Investment, 8, 45, 67, 72, 78, 80, 98, 124, 130, 136, 143, 159, 169
Revenue, 36, 66, 75, 81, 167
Run, 30, 53, 54, 57, 104, 108, 114, 116, 117

S

Safety, 20, 28, 39, 167
Sales, 19, 29, 36, 81, 111, 164
Savings, 61, 78, 79, 81, 99, 118, 119, 122, 124, 126, 127, 130, 132, 133, 136, 138, 139, 143, 167
Schedule, 22, 28, 30, 54, 73, 74, 83, 87, 102, 112
Service, 21, 40, 60, 125, 131, 136, 142, 161, 162, 164, 165
Set-up, 11, 58, 59, 124, 125, 130, 131, 169
Spirit, 1, 4, 146, 160
Spreadsheets, 61, 86, 87, 90
Stand Alone, 169
Standard, 49, 50, 51, 169
Standard Cost, 50, 51
Start-Up, 54, 108, 110, 114, 115, 116
State of the Art, 98
Strategy, 12, 28, 33, 70, 125, 147, 160, 169
Sunk, 169
Supplier, 21, 22, 23, 24, 42, 43, 54, 59, 60, 64, 87, 101, 110, 111, 112, 115, 116
Supplies, 8, 16, 46, 47, 48, 52, 56, 60, 65, 81, 99, 163
Supply, 6, 20, 64
Support, 5, 10, 19, 21, 28, 29, 30, 40, 41, 46, 52, 72, 74, 75, 85, 91, 101, 113, 114, 115, 122, 124, 143, 164, 165

System, 12, 19, 27, 28, 30, 36, 39, 41, 48, 49, 50, 53, 54, 57, 61, 64, 65, 66, 67, 70, 73, 74, 75, 77, 87, 88, 89, 90, 101, 103, 108, 109, 110, 111, 113, 114, 115, 116, 117, 118, 122, 123, 124, 125, 126, 127, 129, 130, 131, 132, 133, 135, 136, 137, 138, 139, 141, 143, 157, 161, 163, 165, 167, 168

T

Tax, 10, 11, 54, 71, 72, 73, 78, 79, 118, 124, 127, 130, 133, 136, 139, 166
Taxable Income, 71, 72, 169
Technology, 4, 5, 6, 10, 11, 16, 21, 23, 28, 32, 43, 48, 53, 75, 87, 89, 102, 104, 108, 113, 114, 124, 125, 130, 131, 136, 137, 142, 149, 166
Tender Loving Care, 169
Thruput, 8, 30, 66, 169
Tooling, 23, 24, 50, 56, 57, 73, 81, 103, 116, 124, 148, 164, 169
Training, 5, 30, 75, 76, 81, 101, 103, 108, 110, 114, 149

U

Utilization, 8, 11, 22, 25, 33, 37, 45, 54, 56, 61, 67, 80, 85, 87, 104, 117, 124, 126, 130, 132, 136, 138, 142, 148, 159, 169

V

Value, 6, 7, 8, 11, 16, 20, 22, 23, 33, 36, 46, 47, 56, 57, 58, 60, 65, 75, 98, 101, 126, 132, 138, 161, 162, 164, 165, 167, 168, 170
Value Added, 1, 57, 170
Variable, 33, 46, 47, 49, 60, 61, 62, 67, 116
Variable Cost, 49, 170
Variance, 51
Vendor, 21, 22, 24, 65, 85, 110, 111
Verify, 30, 55, 56, 117, 165
Volume, 21, 22, 25, 41

W

Work In Process, 124, 125, 130, 131, 170

Must reading for:

> **Equipment Builders**
> **Production Managers**
> **Manufacturing Engineers**
> **Equipment Sellers**
> **Finance People**
> **Executives**
> **Educators**
> **Students**

LEARN how to identify the many opportunities (often disguised as problems) that can make **your** enterprise more productive and profitable.

Actual examples of advanced metal removal, fabrication, and robot welding systems that are operational and proven are included.

Logical arguments that you can use to help justify major capital improvement programs.

Many standard industry concepts are discussed in detail, such as:

> **Thruput**
> **Utilization**
> **Productivity**
> **Program Justification**
> **Automation & Robotics**
> **Return On Investment**
> **Make Or Buy**

UNLEASH YOUR PRODUCTIVITY!